YOU ARE
THE REF

An Hachette UK Company
www.hachette.co.uk

First published in Great Britain in 2018 by Cassell,
an imprint of Octopus Publishing Group Ltd
Carmelite House
50 Victoria Embankment
London EC4Y 0DZ
www.octopusbooks.co.uk

ISBN 978-1-78840-075-6

A CIP catalogue record for this book is available from the
British Library.

Printed and bound in China

10 9 8 7 6 5 4 3 2 1

Publishing Director: Trevor Davies
Editor: Cathy Meeus
Junior Editor: Ella Parsons
Art Director: Juliette Norsworthy
Designer: Hugh Schermuly
Senior Production Manager: Peter Hunt

YOU ARE THE REF

300 footballing conundrums for you to solve

Paul Trevillion & Keith Hackett

CASSELL
ILLUSTRATED

Video Assistant Referee

How VAR will operate – a referee's insight

The International Football Association Board (IFAB) unanimously approved the use of video assistant referee (VAR) technology at its 132nd Annual General Meeting (AGM), which took place in March 2018. Since the beginning of the experiment in the use of VAR in leagues around the world began in March 2016, IFAB reported that the accuracy of reviewable decisions had increased by 5.8 per cent to 98.9 per cent. Along with other data, these results supported the decision to allow VAR to operate around the world in leagues that permit its introduction.

Benefits and limitations

The IFAB criteria are designed to ensure that the use of VAR involves MINIMUM INTERFERENCE in the flow of play, and MAXIMUM BENEFIT to the quality of decision-making. It is to be used only to identify CLEAR AND OBVIOUS ERRORS.

All stakeholders in the game must recognise that the VAR system is not perfect and cannot clarify those grey areas that will always exist in the game of football. The referee always takes the final decision, but should make use of

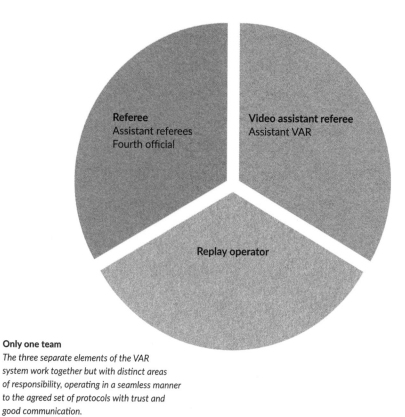

Referee
Assistant referees
Fourth official

Video assistant referee
Assistant VAR

Replay operator

Only one team
The three separate elements of the VAR system work together but with distinct areas of responsibility, operating in a seamless manner to the agreed set of protocols with trust and good communication.

VAR in the same way that he makes use of the contributions of the assistant referees and the fourth official.

Areas of operation

In matches using VAR technology there must be a video operation room (VOR), where the video assistant referee (VAR), assistant VAR (AVAR) and replay operator (RO) work, and at least one referee review area (RRA), where the referee can undertake an on-field review (OFR).

The VOR may be in or close to the stadium or in a more distant location. Only authorised persons are permitted to enter the VOR or to communicate with the VAR, AVAR or RO during the match. A player, substitute or substituted player who enters the VOR will be sent off; a team official who enters the VOR will be dismissed from the technical area.

The RRA must be in a visible location outside the field of play and clearly marked. Any player, substitute or substituted player who enters the RRA will be cautioned. A team official who enters the RRA will be given an official warning (or cautioned).

When VAR can be used

VAR technology will be permitted in order to review incidents in key match-changing situations in four specific situations:

Goals

Penalty kick

Red Cards

Mistaken identity

When reviewing decisions, the team of officials will ask the following questions as relevant in each of these categories:

Goals
- Attacking offence
  Was a foul committed in the lead up to the goal by an attacking player? There is some room for debate as to how far

OFFSIDE

back in the lead up this can be reviewed. Further clarification from IFAB may be needed.
- Offside
  Was an attacking player offside? The assistant referee should delay raising the flag for offside to ensure that when the review takes place an inaccurate flag does not rule out a valid goal.

BALL OUT OF PLAY

SERIOUS
FOUL PLAY

Red cards
- Level of foul
  Was the nature of the foul sufficiently serious to merit a straight red card – i.e. serious foul play, violent conduct, or denial of an obvious goal-scoring opportunity?

- Ball out of play
  Did the ball go out of play in the lead-up up to the goal?

Penalty kick
- Defensive foul
  Did the incident involve a foul by the defending team?
- Location of the foul
  Did the foul take place inside the penalty area?

LOCATION OF THE FOUL

RED CARD SHOWN

Mistaken identity

- Sanction applied to the correct player
  Has the referee correctly identified the player responsible for the foul? The video assistant referee needs to be alert and to intervene verbally over the communication kit to avoid the referee issuing either a red or yellow card to the wrong player.

MISTAKEN
IDENTITY

TREVILLION

VAR in action

On the field of play the referee must verbally communicate with the VAR team to explain the reason for the following decisions:

- To award or not award **PENALTY KICK**.
- To show or not show a **RED CARD** (not including a red card following a second yellow card).
- To award or not award a goal.

Stopping play

- The referee must always be ready to stop the game quickly in case of clear missed incident.
- If the referee seeks the involvement of VAR, play must be halted and must not restart while checks and reviews are in progress.
- If the referee needs to delay the restart of the game because the VAR is being utilised, the referee indicates this to the players and spectators by means of a clear signal. To request a VAR check, the referee will hold a finger to one ear and extend the other hand/arm. To request a VAR review, the referee indicates that an incident will be reviewed by making a square shape.

REQUESTING A VAR CHECK

REQUESTING A VAR REVIEW

Checks and reviews

Only the referee can initiate a review and at the end of the review process, the referee will make the review sign again before the final decision is indicated. The VAR will automatically 'check' all incidents using the broadcaster's footage.

The referee must delay blowing the whistle following an apparent goal if the assistant referee raises the flag in order to enable VAR to check.

Cancelling a red card

- Following a VAR review of the incident, the player should be requested by the referee to join him.
- The referee partly shows the red card and clearly indicates that it has been withdrawn using a crossed arms signal.
- The fourth official advises the team coaches and a public announcement is then made.

CANCELLING A RED CARD

TREVILLION -

MAKING AN INAPPROPRIATE REVIEW REQUEST

Inappropriate review requests

- Players and substitutes who clearly and aggressively make the TV sign must be shown a yellow card.
- Team officials or coaches who clearly and aggressively make the TV sign must be warned.
- Players or team officials who enter the referee review area (RRA), where the VAR equipment is sited near the field of play, must be shown a yellow card.

Review after play has restarted

VAR cannot be used following the restart of play for missed penalty decisions, serious foul play, or for missed offside rulings. It can, however, be used after the restart of play in the case of direct red card offences involving violent conduct, spitting, biting and extremely offensive, insulting or abusive gestures. These offences will always be reviewed by the referee in the RRA. VAR cannot be reviewed for use of offensive language.

Half-time and full-time whistle

To avoid players leaving the field of play, the referee should not whistle to end the period of play if a reviewable incident happens at the end of the first half or at full time and a check or review is needed.

PLAYERS AND TEAM OFFICIALS ENTERING THE REFEREE REVIEW AREA

TREVILLION -

VAR and assistant referees

The use of VAR has several implications for the way in which assistant referees signal their observations.

- In most cases, the assistant referee should delay raising the offside flag if a player is in a very good scoring position – for example, the player is in or close to the penalty area or moving with a free run with a direct goal-scoring opportunity. However, the assistant referee should raise the flag immediately if convinced that the player is offside.
- The assistant referee should communicate his opinion to the referee when the action is concluded to contribute to the VAR review.
- The assistant referee should raise the flag only when the situation is concluded by a goal, corner or continuation of play.
- The assistant referee is encouraged to delay raising the flag to ensure that the ball has gone out of play (especially over the goal line) before play is halted.

AN ASSISTANT SHARES HIS OPINION
WITH THE REFEREE

Video assistant referee and assistant VAR

The video assistant referee watches the live match and also a screen that operates with a three-second delay. The assistant VAR continues to watch the live game while a check is taking place in case another incident occurs. The video assistant referee needs to communicate directly with other members of the refereeing team in the following situations:

- **Marking**. Where the video assistant referee indicates to the operator that a video clip of a specific incident should be saved.
- **Silent check**. Where the referee and the video assistant referee communicate privately.
- **Alert check** with **Communication**. Where a check is in progress – for example, for a penalty kick or for a red card.
- **Stop play** and **Delay restart**. Where conferring with the referee on stopping or restarting play following a reviewable incident.
- **Initiate a review**. Where the referee requests a review.

The video assistant referee can intervene to suggest a review or stoppage in the following situations:

- Referee has shown a second yellow card but failed to dismiss the player.
- The referee appears to have mistaken the identity of a player who is to receive a yellow or red card.
- A team has more players on the field of play than the number permitted.
- A team is about to kick off without a goalkeeper.
- A player is bleeding or appears to be seriously injured.

Spectator awareness

Educating the football spectators in the operation of VAR technology and the rules surrounding its use is important for its acceptance and for the smooth and orderly conduct of matches in which it is used. The Professional Referee Organization (PRO) manages referees operating in Major League Soccer in the United States and have been very pro-active in supporter education and have produced a number of resources and introduced a number of practices that may be of use in easing the adoption of VAR in the game throughout the world:

- An online video explanation of how VAR operates.
- This video explanation is also played in stadiums before matches.
- When a VAR review is in process a stadium announcement is made.
- A replay is shown to spectators once play has resumed.

STADIUM ANNOUNCEMENT

TREVILLION -

THE QUESTIONS

Your assistant wrongly flags an inactive player offside, so you allow play to continue. However, the ball, which had been heading out of play, strikes the raised flag and bounces into the path of another attacker, who is in an onside position, and who races away with it. What now?

1

At the final whistle, a sniggering striker trots over to an opposition defender who had scored a bizarre hat-trick of own goals and tries to give him the match ball. The defender reacts by flipping the ball back up into the striker's face. You intervene as they square up. Both players are on yellow cards. What now?

2

At a corner, a defender is marking a striker closely. The striker attempts to wind up the defender by kissing him on the cheek. The defender reacts angrily and pushes the striker to the ground. What action do you take?

5

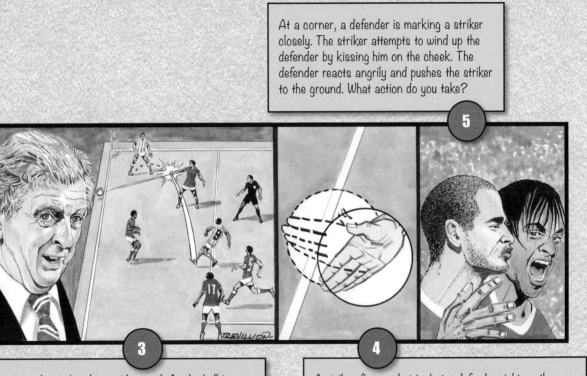

3

The away side are breaking with speed. As the ball is played forwards into the box, the last defender deliberately punches it away just before it reaches an opposition striker, who was standing in an offside position. Do you penalise the defender or signal for offside?

4

A striker fires a shot in, but a defender right on the edge of the box deliberately blocks it with his hand. The sheer power of the shot forces the defender's hand back into the penalty area. The ball was in contact with his hand both in and out of the area. Is it a penalty?

The players in a wall, lined up to face a left-footed free kick, suddenly reposition themselves when a right-footed player runs up instead. They move sideways away from your foam line, and when the ball is deflected to safety, the attackers demand a retake. What now?

6

You signal for a player to come back onto the pitch after injury, but as he puts one foot back in play, he sees an opponent kick a clearance towards him. He steps back, catches the ball and takes a quick throw. Do you intervene?

8

7

A striker races into the penalty area and takes a theatrical dive to evade a reckless tackle by a defender. No contact was made. Both are on a yellow card. What do you do?

In a penalty area melée you spot a bookable offence, and think the guilty party was the home side's new star signing, who is already on a yellow card. But before you act, one of his teammates dashes up and tells you you've got it wrong and owns up to the foul himself. What now?

9

A sub races on to the pitch before the player he is replacing has left the field, but suddenly pulls up with a torn hamstring. His manager wants to cancel the switch. Do you let him?

11

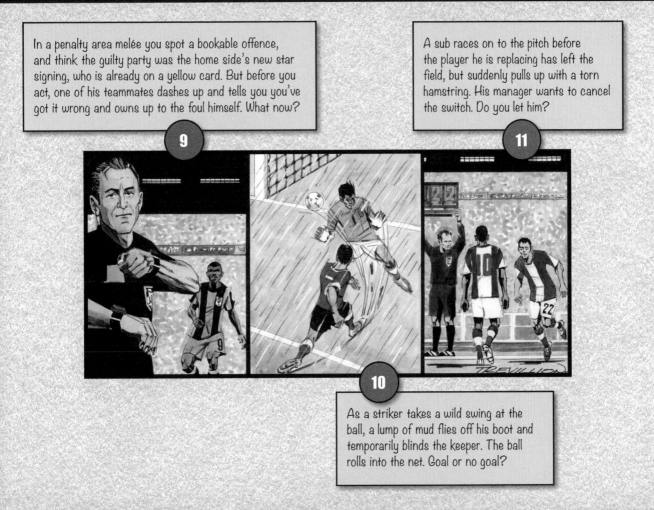

10

As a striker takes a wild swing at the ball, a lump of mud flies off his boot and temporarily blinds the keeper. The ball rolls into the net. Goal or no goal?

13 A keeper receives a back pass and tries to dribble his way out of trouble. But, after beating one challenge realises the risk he is taking, so – still just inside his area – he drops on the ball instead. Play on?

14 On a rain-drenched pitch a player taking a corner slips and kicks the flag post first then the ball. The ball rolls ten yards away and is cleared up field, but you spot the flag and the post are now lying on the pitch. Do you intervene?

12 The home manager is serving a one-game stadium ban. But during the first half you notice the home side's bear mascot is angrily jumping up and down on the touchline shouting instructions to the home players. His voice sounds familiar. What now?

A player on a yellow card is clearly tripped by an opponent – but before you can blow for the foul he picks the ball up, ready to take a quick free kick. What now?

16

As a corner kick flies into a crowded penalty area, you spot three simultaneous offences: two defenders deliberately dragging down the attackers they are marking, and a third attacker shoving his marker in the face. There's uproar. What now?

17

15

You're surprised to see a defender duck out of a header, leaving a striker to score unchallenged. The defender and the keeper are furious, saying the striker shouted, 'leave it', mimicking the keeper's distinctive accent. What do you do?

At half time the home manager grabs you and insists you watch a replay of the away side's goal on a fan's phone. The video shows the striker clearly handling the ball into the net. What's worse, it also shows the striker surreptitiously giving thumbs up to your assistant, who slyly nods back. What do you do?

Inside his own penalty area, a full-back passes to his centre-back, who slips and falls. Spotting the danger, the keeper picks up the loose ball before a nearby striker can reach it. What now?

19

20

TREVILLION—

18

The defending team makes a substitution before a corner kick is taken, replacing one centre-back with another. But before the new player has arrived in the box, you signal for the kick to be taken and an unmarked striker scores. There's uproar. What now?

The ball is nodded clear from a crowded penalty area, only to be volleyed straight back in again. The shot flies towards a striker, who is clearly in an offside position, but he jumps out of the way and the ball flies into the net. Your assistant flags. What now?

21

Before a big match you're surprised to see one of your assistants arrive at the ground wearing the away side's replica top. You challenge him and he tells you he's a lifelong supporter, but it will not affect his judgement. Do you intervene?

23

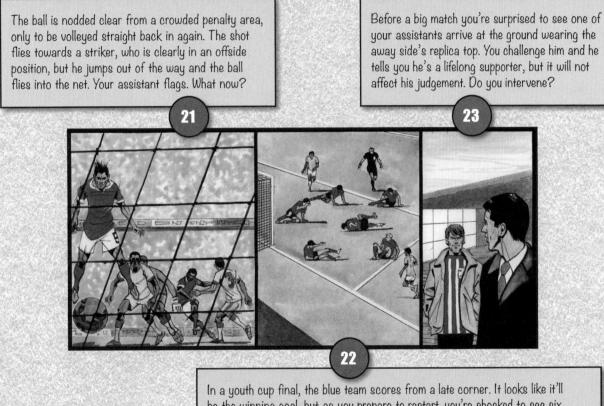

22

In a youth cup final, the blue team scores from a late corner. It looks like it'll be the winning goal, but as you prepare to restart, you're shocked to see six defenders throw themselves to the floor, all claiming serious injury. Their manager then marches on to demand an abandonment and a replay. What do you do?

A maverick striker is furious to be subbed and after he steps off the pitch, he kicks the player who has replaced him. The substitute, who had one foot on the pitch, is now too injured to come on, and his side have used all their subs. What do you do?

24

In a sudden counterattack a midfielder plays the ball forward to a teammate who is inside his own half, and clean through on goal. But your assistant flags for offside, and the striker stops, shouting in outrage. What now?

25

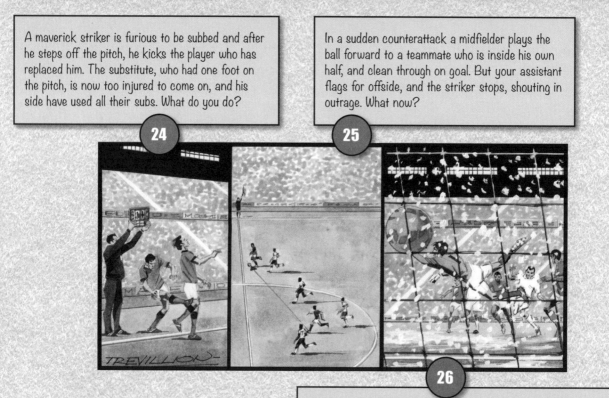

26

There are patches of snow on the pitch and wintry flurries in the air. After 20 minutes, the away team in their all-white strip go 2–0 up. The home manager storms onto the pitch, complaining that his players can't see the opposition clearly. What now?

In the 87th minute of a freezing, wet non-league game, at 3–0 up, the home side loses a player to injury. None of the subs want to come on, so the home manager voluntarily goes down to ten men. But when the opposition scores, he demands the right to send on one of his subs after all. What do you do?

27

A player with a reputation for diving, already on a yellow card, is kicked in the chest. You think he dived, but as you show him a second yellow, he tears off his shirt to reveal some nasty stud marks. What now?

29

28

In the opening minute of a game you fail to spot that both your assistants are operating in the same half of the pitch. You only notice when a goal is scored, and one of them flags for offside, while the other does not. What do you do?

The keeper tries to clear a back pass but scuffs his kick. The ball flies up, bounces on the 18-yard line, and spins back into his arms before a striker can reach it. What now?

30

A game goes to penalties. The away manager, worried that he has an inexperienced keeper in goal, sends his goalkeeping coach to stand behind the net and shout advice. Do you intervene?

32

GO RIGHT!

TREVILLION-

31

In the dying seconds of a 7–0 cup thrashing, two opponents decide to call it a day: they change shirts early and shake hands laughing. But then the ball breaks towards them, and the home striker, wearing an away top, smacks the ball into the net. Goal or no goal?

The red team's star player fires a thunderous shot at goal. It beats the keeper and is clearly going in until it smacks an unfortunate teammate in the face. As the teammate collapses in his offside position, the ball rebounds to another, clearly onside red team colleague, who slots it into the net. Goal or no goal?

In the last game of the season, the away side need a point to stay up while the home side are already safe and feeling relaxed. At half time you spot some empty champagne bottles in the home team's dressing room and the players admit they've had a glass or two each. What now?

33

34

A manager who has used all his subs has a furious half-time bust up with his team captain. He tells you he has sacked the captain and will voluntarily finish the game with ten men. But the captain and his teammates tell you to ignore the manager. They say he has 'lost the plot' and want to start the second half as normal. What do you do?

In a swift counterattack, a player, supported by a teammate, has a clear run at goal. But just as he's about to shoot, his teammate on a hat-trick, gives him a hard shove off the ball and scores instead. What now?

35

37

36

In a penalty shoot-out, all the outfield players score from their kicks, so the keepers are up next. But when the first keeper scuffs his kick wide, the second keeper dashes out and smacks him in the face. He clearly wants to be sent off so that his side's star striker can take the kick instead of him. There's uproar. What now?

After a goalmouth scramble, an opposition striker sportingly helps the keeper back to his feet. But as he does so, he lets go, the keeper tumbles back over the line and spills the ball into the net. The striker wheels away to celebrate. Goal or no goal?

38

During a substitution, the fourth official holds up his board signalling for number 9 to come off. But after the change is complete, the player's manager, who was busy talking to his staff, realises the wrong player has come off.
You approach your colleague, who sheepishly admits he pressed the wrong button. What now?

39

40

You play advantage after a foul. But when the player in possession kicks a long ball up field, it accidentally strikes a teammate and rebounds over his own keeper into the net. Is it an own goal?

In a fierce bad-tempered relegation battle with tackles flying in and both teams down to ten men, a striker goes through on goal with only one defender to beat. But as the defender races in to make a tackle, the shin pad on his leading leg flies out of his sock. What now?

41

After a clash of heads, a groggy defender gets up and signals his opponent needs treatment. But as he does so and before you can stop play, he accidentally back heels the ball into his own net. Goal or no goal?

43

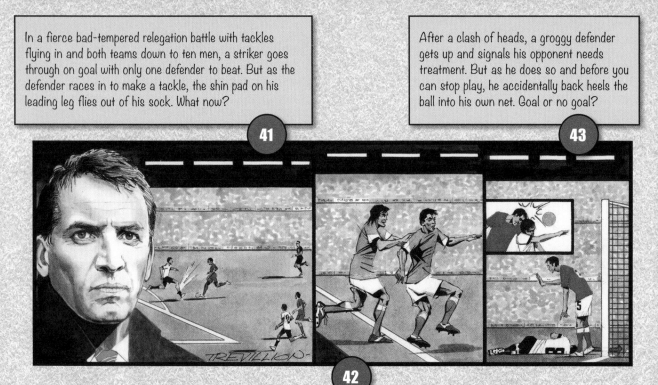

TREVILLION

42

A famously volatile player is substituted moments after you book him. As he walks off, you hear him make swearing and abusive comments in your direction – but before you can react, he quickly steps over the line and pushes his replacement onto the field of play. The substitution is complete. What do you do?

A player is off balance as he stretches to strike a volley, so he steadies himself by leaning on you. The brief contact is enough to keep him upright and he lashes the ball into the net. Goal or no goal?

44

It's the final day of the season with all the games due to kick off simultaneously. But at your match, where the home side need to win by a certain number of goals to stay up, depending on other results, an apparent power failure has jammed the turnstiles. Club officials insist it willl take at least an hour to fix. But you suspect it is a ruse to gain an advantage. Do you delay the game, postpone it, or start on time?

46

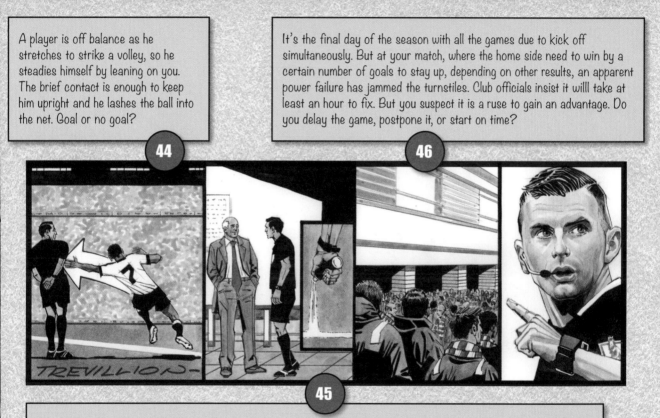

TREVILLION

45

You warn a manager at half time that you've had enough of his players trying to surround and intimidate you every time there's a close decision. You tell him that for the rest of the game, at any such incident you will spray a line four feet in front of yourself and book any player who crosses it. He laughs and tells you you've lost control. What now?

A defender makes a rash, badly timed tackle on the touchline, but insists he was distracted by the vivid electronic pitch-side advert, which features a pile of bouncing footballs. What do you do?

47

A veteran striker is flagging badly, but suddenly perks up after receiving treatment from the physio. When he scores five minutes later, the fourth official calls you over and he tells you he saw the physio giving the striker what appeared to be strong black coffee. What now?

48

49

During the half-time break, you are made aware by officials that a player you booked earlier had placed a bet on himself to pick up a yellow card before the break. Do you let him return for the second half?

At a throw-in a defender hurls the ball back to his keeper. But the keeper fails to control it. As the ball slips under his foot, he dives backwards in an effort to stop it going into his goal, but only succeeds in pushing it into the net. Do you award the opposition a free kick because he handled the ball, give an own goal, or do something else?

50

A striker goes sprawling in the penalty area, apparently brought down by the last man. But as you reach for your red card, the striker springs up and sportingly admits there was no contact. This prompts his captain to intervene, dragging the striker away and telling you to award the penalty kick and the red card. What now?

52

51

A keeper tries to launch a kick up field, but it cannons into the back of a striker on the edge of the penalty area, rebounds and goes into the net. Is it a goal?

A shot flies towards the home side's net for what could be the winner, when a ball boy hurls a spare ball into its path. One ball goes into the net; the other deflects over the bar. You've no idea which was which. What next?

53

When you award a penalty in a heated derby, a player behind you unleashes a loud torrent of abuse in your direction. But when you turn round you see three players together, all looking innocent. They all deny saying anything. What action do you take?

54

A defender leaps to try to clear a whipped-in cross. The ball clearly strikes his outstretched arm, but his eyes were tightly shut as he jumped. What is your decision?

55

In the final minute of the final game of the season, there's a party atmosphere. A draw means the home side will stay up, and the away side will win the title. The players annoy you by juggling the ball between them to run down the clock, and when it hits you, you instinctively kick it away. You then watch horrified as the ball flies into the home side's net. Everyone freezes. Goal or no goal?

56

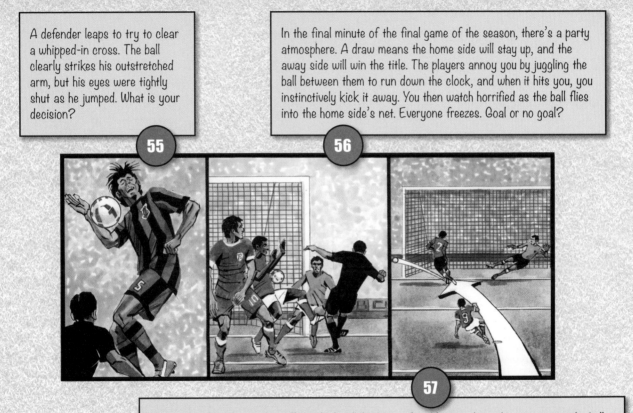

57

A penalty-taker slips and scuffs his kick. While the confused keeper dives the wrong way, the ball slowly rolls towards the empty left corner of the net. But before it crosses the line, the defender, who entered the area legitimately after the kick was taken, manages to clear it away. What now?

Three goals down after 20 minutes, the home side are raging, blaming your decisions for all the goals. The captain and manager both say that unless you hand over to the fourth official, they'll walk off. What now?

58

Just before a through ball is played towards the away side's star striker, his marker deliberately barges him into an offside position. The striker reacts brilliantly, somehow regaining his balance and racing clear. What action do you take?

60

59

When you book a player late in the game for a dirty tackle, he loses control and starts to storm off the pitch in protest. But just before he crosses the line, his manager signals that he'll substitute him. What now?

A striker scuffs the vital kick in a penalty shoot-out, sending the ball trickling goalwards. The keeper reacts by racing off his line and booting it away in celebration only for it to hit you and ricochet back into the net. Everyone freezes. What do you do?

61

You award a penalty, but the swirling wind means the ball won't stay on the spot and, as it's an artificial pitch, the penalty taker cannot make a divot to keep it in place. What now?

63

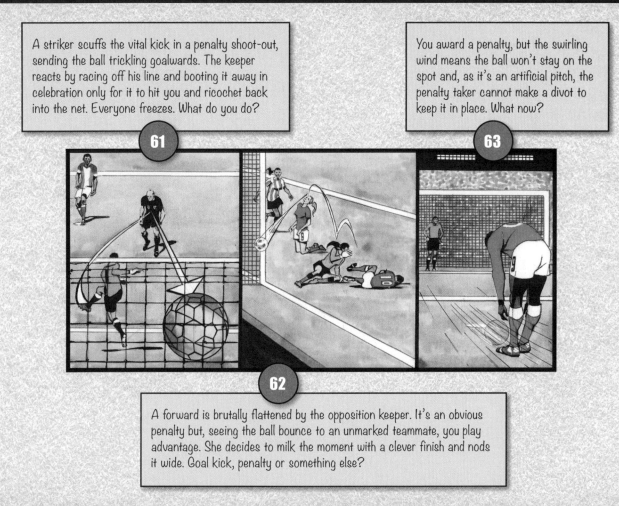

62

A forward is brutally flattened by the opposition keeper. It's an obvious penalty but, seeing the ball bounce to an unmarked teammate, you play advantage. She decides to milk the moment with a clever finish and nods it wide. Goal kick, penalty or something else?

The home manager sends his keeper up for a last-ditch corner. When the ball is hoofed clear up field, you start blowing the final whistle, but as you get to the second of your three peeps, you see the ball bouncing into the home side's empty net. There's uproar. What's your decison?

64

A midfielder launches a strike in the dying seconds of a rainy non-league game. It hits the underside of the bar and appears to go in before bouncing clear. But the goal line has disappeared in the wet, churned-up mud. Players swarm around you. What now?

66

65

In the 90th minute the attacking team take a quick throw next to their opponents' corner flag. The taker then sprints along the goal line, still off the pitch, and when the cross comes in, he re-enters the field of play near the post and heads the ball into the net. Goal or no goal?

The last defender makes a clean tackle on the edge of the area and ends up in a heap with the striker. Spotting another forward racing on to the loose ball, which has stopped right on the 18-yard line, the defender swipes it away with his hand. What do you do?

67

TREVILLION

68

A player emerges for the second half wearing glasses. He explains that his contact lenses kept falling out. What do you do?

69

A defender and a striker sprint into the area. Although the ball remains in play, both players end up sliding out over the goal line, where the defender fouls his opponent. The striker isn't hurt but the defender is able to get up faster and clears the ball. What now?

70 As a red team striker dribbles into his opponent's penalty area, you suddenly notice a major disturbance at the other end: two red team defenders punching each other inside their own area. What action do you take?

72 As two opponents square up to each other, the defender, standing just outside the penalty area, spits at the striker, who is just inside it. What do you do?

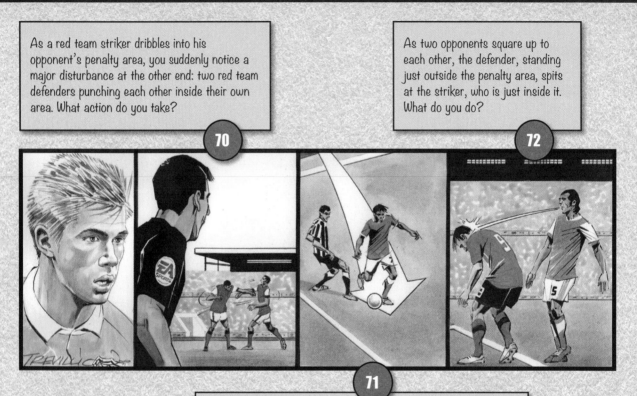

71 A defender is waiting for you to wave him back on to the pitch after receiving treatment. But when he spots an opponent break clean through on goal, he races back on without permission, tackles the striker cleanly and clears the ball to safety. What now?

After a fierce but fair melée in the box the ball drops to a striker. Before he can tap it into the net, a defender stops it with his hand, and then points to blood trickling down his face. What do you do?

74

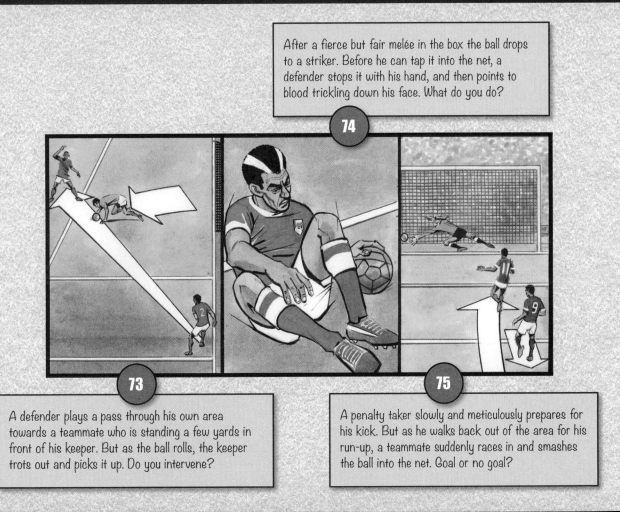

73

A defender plays a pass through his own area towards a teammate who is standing a few yards in front of his keeper. But as the ball rolls, the keeper trots out and picks it up. Do you intervene?

75

A penalty taker slowly and meticulously prepares for his kick. But as he walks back out of the area for his run-up, a teammate suddenly races in and smashes the ball into the net. Goal or no goal?

During half time you are made aware that a group of subs who have been warming up on the pitch are fighting each other. When you make it outside you find one of them on the ground with a head wound. A television producer says it has all been caught on camera. What now?

76

A defender slips, gifting a striker an easy scoring chance. But as the striker shoots, the defender puts his hand between the boot and the ball. The striker kicks the hand on to the ball, and the shot flies wide. As the defender screams in agony, both sides protest. What do you do?

77

78

A keeper parries a direct free kick to a striker who was standing in the defensive wall. But when the striker scores from the rebound, your assistant flags for offside. The attacker is furious, pointing out that he was only offside because the wall edged forwards over your foam line as the shot was struck. He's right. Goal or no goal?

A keeper handles outside the box, but you play advantage, allowing a nearby striker to knock the ball into the empty net. But as his shot rolls goalwards, a teammate in an offside position nips in and applies the finishing touch. What do you do?

79

The last player to take his turn in an epic penalty shoot-out loses his nerve. He says he's afraid he'll blow his chance to equalise, and refuses to take his kick. What is your response?

80

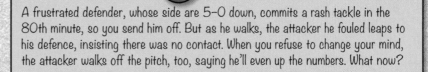

81

A frustrated defender, whose side are 5–0 down, commits a rash tackle in the 80th minute, so you send him off. But as he walks, the attacker he fouled leaps to his defence, insisting there was no contact. When you refuse to change your mind, the attacker walks off the pitch, too, saying he'll even up the numbers. What now?

At the coin toss before a local derby, the two captains refuse to shake hands, and instead aim insults at each other. Before you can react, they start throwing punches. What now?

83

A striker volleys a loose clearance towards the empty net. But before the ball crosses the line, a desperate ball boy races on, dives across goal, and manages to tip it on to the post. The striker slams home the rebound. Goal or no goal?

84

82

The ball is punted out by an away team player, but just as it goes over the line, the home manager, who is standing on the pitch, leaps to catch it. He tosses it to one of his players for a quick throw. What do you do?

A veteran star player, who pledged to strip to his pants for charity if he scored in his farewell match, finds the net seconds before half time. As you prepare to blow for the break, he dashes off down the tunnel, stripping as he goes. He's already on a yellow card. What do you do?

85

During a downpour, a defender recklessly slides in to intercept a pass. The striker nearest the ball has time to get out of the way, but knowing the defender is already on a yellow card, he chooses not to. As he tumbles, he waves on imaginary card at you. What now?

86

87

After a melée in the muddy six-yard area, your wrist monitor buzzes to signal that the ball has gone in. You've no idea how or who scored it, but you award a goal. As you do so, though, the incensed keeper rushes over. He insists the scorer slapped it in, and shows you a man-sized handprint on the otherwise filthy ball. What now?

A header hits the left post, the right post, and then bounces back into the field of play. You are 100 per cent certain it did not cross the line, but your wrist monitor buzzes to signal it did. What now?

88

Before a penalty, the taker calmly walks towards the keeper, points to a spot 30 cm inside the post, and tells him. 'I'm going to place the ball right there.' He then walks back to take the kick. Do you interfere?

90

89

A striker celebrates a stunning goal by making the sign of a cross and raising his hands in prayer. The beaten keeper is outraged, insisting that the striker has breached IFAB rules on religious messages. What do you do?

You award a last-minute free kick right on the touchline near the dugouts. The taker wants to launch the ball into the penalty area, but the opposition manager stands in the way of his run-up and refuses to budge. He insists he can stand where he wants inside his own technical area. Is he right?

91

You play advantage after a foul, but the midfielder who collects the ball opts to blast it into touch rather than continue the attacking move. He knows his side have a dead-ball specialist, and he wants the free kick, not the advantage. What now?

93

92

The red team look to take a quick throw. The nearest player collects the ball and launches it, but at the same time, a teammate receives a spare ball from a ball boy and hurls that into play too. What action do you take?

Following a foul, you play advantage, planning to book the player at the next stoppage. But the player then commits a second bookable offence. The opposing team appeal for a red card, but the player claims he would never have made such a risky second tackle had he known you were going to book him for the first. What now?

94

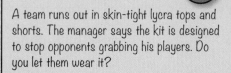

95

A team runs out in skin-tight lycra tops and shorts. The manager says the kit is designed to stop opponents grabbing his players. Do you let them wear it?

96

An indirect free kick is aimed at the home side's star striker. He misses the header, but the tip of his pony tail brushes the ball as it flies into the net. Goal or no goal?

A defender who is trying to block a goal-bound shot suddenly appears to suffer some sort of seizure – flinging an arm out and deflecting the ball wide before collapsing. As you call the physio on, you've no idea whether or not he was faking it. What do you do?

97

Midway through the second half with the home team 5–0 down, the home captain is seriously injured. After an ambulance is called, the home manager tells you that the rest of his team are too traumatised to continue. He wants abandonment. What now?

98

99

On a very slippery surface, a clumsy defender launches himself into a sliding tackle right by the corner of the 18-yard box. Initial contact is made outside the area, but then the foul continues into the penalty area. The pair finally end up sprawled in a heap outside it again. Is this a penalty?

You share a surname with the home team's keeper. When he commits a foul and you award a penalty, his teammates scream foul abuse at him, using his surname. But several of them are looking at you. What do you do?

100

At the coin toss you fumble the catch, but the home captain cleverly picks the coin from the air before it hits the grass, then slaps it on his wrist and asks his opponent to call it. The away captain shouts heads, and heads it is. Both are happy to kick off in the normal way. Are you?

101

102

You accidentally block a defence-splitting pass, so you apologise for your clumsiness. The players seem to have accepted it and play continues, but moments later, the midfielder who had played the pass sends you flying with a brutal 'accidental' body charge. He says, 'Sorry for being so clumsy'. What now?

One of your assistants has churned up his part of the wet pitch so much that he takes to running inside the line when the ball is not nearby. The defenders complain that he's causing a distraction and a danger. Do you intervene?

103

With snow obscuring some of the pitch markings, one of the keepers uses half time to mark out a line with red chalk from his goal line to the penalty spot. He says it's the only way he can judge angles. What action do you take?

104

105

When he nets the ball to give his team a 6–0 lead near the end of a cup semi-final, the scorer takes his shirt off and stands right in front of you celebrating. You realise he wants to be booked now, as it will trigger a suspension for his next league game, removing any risk of being suspended for the final. Do you book him?

A defender badly scuffs a back pass sending the ball towards his own net. The horrified keeper makes a desperate attempt to stop it, but ends up heading the ball onto his post, then tipping the rebound over the bar with his hand. What do you do?

A striker is frustrated by a defender going to ground too early, trying to win a free kick- so he tries hauling him to his feet. But as he does so the ball is fired back into the box. It rebounds off the defender, who is playing the striker onside and the striker scores. What do you do?

107

108

106

When his side concede a third goal, their manager, who is under pressure, storms out of his dugout and up into the television commentary box, where he punches a famously critical pundit. He then returns to the dugout. Do you intervene?

A goalkeeper accidentally collides with a defender and an opposition striker. While medical staff see to them, the striker's captain insists that all three players should leave the field before play restarts. What action do you take?

109

A half-time sub scores and whips off his shirt in celebration. But as you go to book him. You realise he's the same player who was substituted in the first half after you booked him. He has come back on wearing someone else's shirt. What now?

110

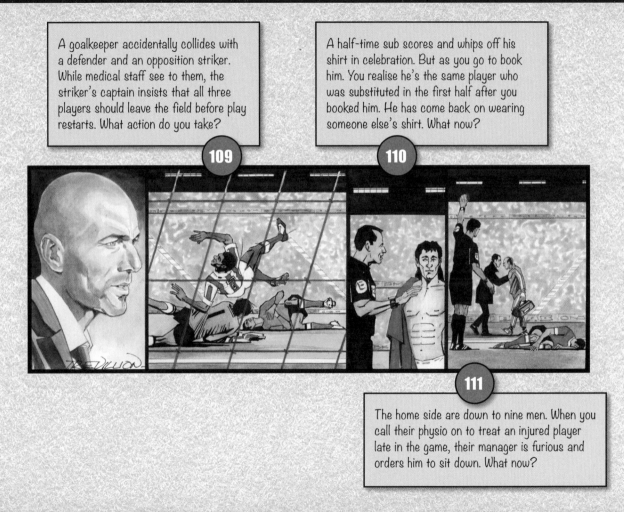

111

The home side are down to nine men. When you call their physio on to treat an injured player late in the game, their manager is furious and orders him to sit down. What now?

In a bad-tempered match, two players from the home team go down injured, so the away side's physio comes on to help. But as he arrives, the home keeper suddenly puts his hands to his face in apparent pain. He says the physio deliberately aimed a burst of freeze spray into his face as he ran past. His eyes are clearly red. What now?

112

A defender, already on a yellow, takes his side's ninth penalty in a penalty shoot-out and skies it. In his anger he turns and kicks at the penalty spot, gouging a hole in the pitch. The opposition are outraged, and refuse to take their potentially decisive kick until he is sent off and the surface re-laid. What is your decision?

114

113

A defender attempts to head a corner over the bar to safety, but it deflects off his man-bun and into his own net. When the ball made contact, the man-bun flew off, revealing itself to be a clip-on. Does the goal stand?

It's 1–1 in the last minute when a wayward shot heads straight for your face. Instinctively you swat it away and watch in horror as it flies into the net. Goal or no goal?

115

A controversial manager is serving a two-game stadium ban. But as you walk past his side's dressing room before kick-off, you see him on a big screen giving a team talk to his players via a webcam. Do you intervene?

116

117

During a European cup game the home players complain they are being racially abused by away fans and threaten to walk off. But the chant could be innocent – the away side's star striker has a surname that sounds rather like a racial slur. You're not sure what's really happening. What do you do?

Late in the second half you ask a player with blood on his shirt to leave the pitch and change it. As play continues, he grabs a new shirt and races back on, but in his haste he has put it on inside out, obscuring his name and number. Do you stop play?

118

With a strong wind blowing, a player tries a throw-in down the line. The ball enters the field of play, but isn't touched by anyone else before it is blown back out again. Is it a retake, a foul throw or something else?

120

119

The fourth official calls you over to inspect a substitute's boots. Instead of studs, the boots have special moulded leather strips the same length as studs, but in a new ridged design. Can he come on?

Late on in a rain-drenched game a player taking a corner kick finds the quadrant submerged, so she places the ball on the nearest bit of dry grass instead and plays it short. The opposing team protest. What do you do?

121

In a frantic, edgy game you confuse the numbers you've written down of the players you've booked and, instead of cautioning the number 6 you mistakenly dismiss the number 9 for two yellows. He reacts angrily, ripping the card from your hand and pointing out your mistake. What now?

122

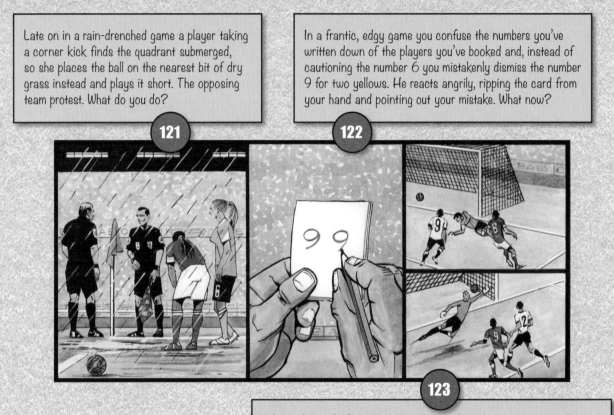

123

After a fierce 3–3 draw, the two hat-trick scorers race over and demand the match ball. The home striker says it's his, as he completed his hat trick first. They start pushing and shoving. What do you do?

A striker who is clean through on goal suddenly pulls up. It looks like a torn hamstring. But when the crouching keeper hesitates and stands up, the striker smashes the ball into the net. It was a ruse. Goal or no goal?

124

A midfielder commits a foul that merits a second yellow card, but you play advantage as the opposition are in on goal. However, when their shot is cleared, it drops straight to the midfielder you planned to book. He turns, races up field and scores. What do you do?

126

125

You break up a row and reprimand two opposing players. You're not sure what sparked it off until half time, when angry home officials show you a television replay of the away player racially abusing their player. What now?

In the last game of the season, the away side need a five-goal win to stay up. But 2-0 down at half time, their owner storms in and dismisses his manager. Players from both sides are outraged, and in the second half the home side deliberately allow their opponents to score repeatedly to bring the tally to 2-8. Do you intervene?

127

In a meaningless end-of-season game the home manager says he wants to kick off with ten men to make a point about his notoriously tight chairman refusing to spend money. He says he will send his 11th player onto the pitch in the 11th minute. Do you let him?

129

128

In stoppage time you award a direct free kick to the home side. The away team, clinging to a 1-0 lead, bring on a sub, and you signal for the kick to be taken. But as the ball flies into the net, you spot the subbed player has not completely left the field of play. What now?

A player receives an accidental knock to the head and ends up in a heap just off the pitch. As the physio races over, the opposition have a scoring chance, so you play on. But as the attack continues, the player rolls back onto the pitch, followed by the physio. What do you do?

130

A keeper pumps the air after apparently making a world-class fingertip save and the opposition race off to take a quick corner. But you don't think he touched it and your assistant just shrugs. What now?

132

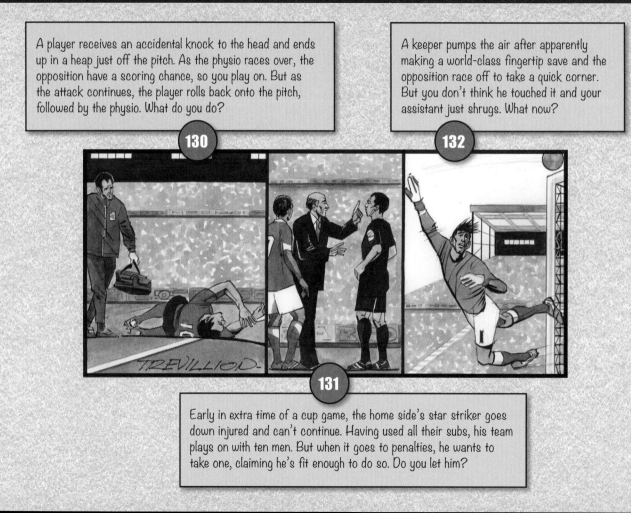

131

Early in extra time of a cup game, the home side's star striker goes down injured and can't continue. Having used all their subs, his team plays on with ten men. But when it goes to penalties, he wants to take one, claiming he's fit enough to do so. Do you let him?

Just before kick-off in a crucial cup game, one of your assistants realises that his ex-wife is playing for the away team. Do you allow him to officiate?

133

In the week before a big local derby, a well-known player makes the brave decision to come out. But during the game he suffers abuse from the terraces and at half time complains that the opposition manager has joined in. What action do you take?

135

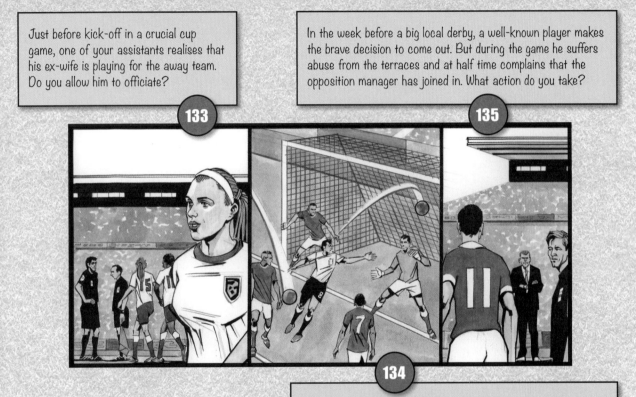

134

In the closing seconds the home crowd refuse to return the ball for a throw-in so the away taker grabs a spare from a ball boy and hurls it into the box. As a striker leaps to head it in, a fan throws the original back into the box. What do you do?

A defender jumps up and down in front of a forward who is trying to take a quick throw. So the attacker throws the ball at him, collects the rebound, races away, and scores. Goal or no goal?

136

A keeper drags down a striker in a one-on-one. You blow your whistle and point to the penalty mark – only to see the ball carry on rolling and end up in the net. Do you now give the goal instead?

138

137

A winger sprinting down the line loses his footing and looks as if he will tumble out of play until he crashes into your assistant. As your colleague is sent flying, the winger regains his balance and whips over a cross to a teammate who looks suspiciously offside. He heads it in. Goal or no goal?

An away player goes down in stoppage time. The home captain, upset by his opponents' constant time wasting, reacts by carrying him off the pitch against his will. His physio objects vociferously. What action do you take?

139

A defender's clearance flies off towards the corner flag and knocks it clean out of its hole. You've no idea whether to give a throw or a corner kick. What do you decide?

141

140

Near the end of a lively cup final, you award a third controversial penalty, this time to the team who are 5–0 down. To your surprise, the fouled player then boots the spot kick wide on purpose. He explains he dived to win the penalty, just to prove you're easily conned. What do you do?

In a goalmouth melée, a striker on the line ferociously blasts the ball at a defender's back, deliberately using him to deflect the ball into the net. The opposing team are furious – some calling for offside, others claiming violent conduct. Goal or no goal?

142

Not long before kick off, the away team's kit man discovered that someone has vandalised the players' names on all of their shirts – and has done the same to their spares. There's uproar. What action do you take?

143

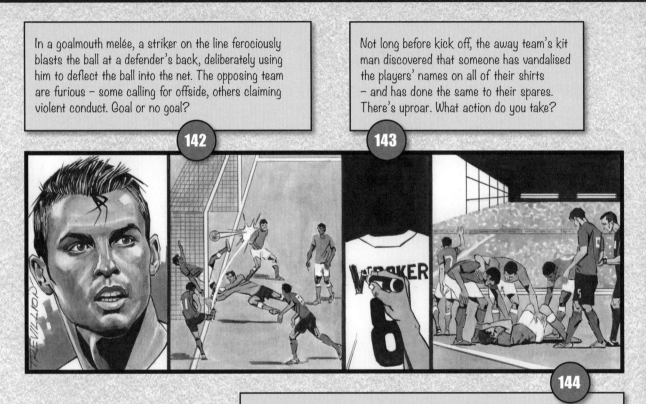

144

A player launches a terrible tackle worthy of a red card, but suffers serious injury in the process. As you try to control the brawl that follows, the medics take off the injured player before you can show a red card, and the fourth official waves through a substitution. What do you do?

Just before the coin toss, the home captain, whom you wrongly sent off earlier in the season, produces a red card from his pocket and waves it at you. His teammates cheer. What do you do?

145

The away side have been blatantly time wasting to hold onto a 0–0 draw, so you signal six extra minutes. The home side scores and demand you blow the final whistle immediately. They say playing the full six minutes would now unfairly reward the away side, by giving them a chance to equalise. Are they right?

147

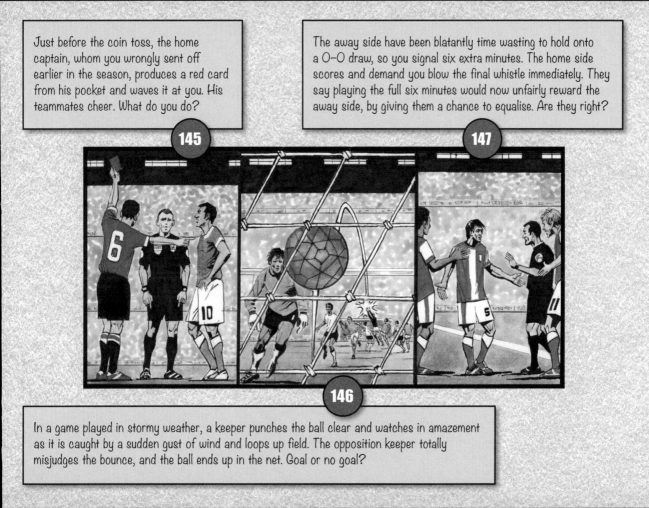

146

In a game played in stormy weather, a keeper punches the ball clear and watches in amazement as it is caught by a sudden gust of wind and loops up field. The opposition keeper totally misjudges the bounce, and the ball ends up in the net. Goal or no goal?

It's a crucial late penalty. The opposition fans behind the goal try to put off the taker, so the attacking side's players, at the edge of the box, try to do the same to the keeper. Do you intervene?

148

A winger racing in from the corner nutmegs the last defender but has to run off the pitch to get past him. The keeper sees this, stops playing and shouts for a free kick. But the winger plays on and rolls the ball into the unguarded net. Goal or no goal?

149

150

The attacking side has an indirect free kick inside the area. The defenders line up on the goal line, but so do the attackers, just in front of them. As the kick is taken, the attackers scatter and in the confusion, the ball flies into the net off a defender. The defending team are furious, saying they were impeded and couldn't see. What do you do?

You're an inexperienced ref in your first senior game. The home side's veteran captain repeatedly questions your decisions. When you tell him to stop, he says he is allowed to talk to you throughout. He has not used any abusive language. What do you do next?

151

A striker chases the ball towards the corner. He reaches it, but as he does so, he slides off the pitch, grabbing the corner flag post behind him and bending it to stop the ball dribbling out of play. In a flash he is back on his feet and manages to whip in a cross to a striker who heads the ball into the net. Is it a goal?

153

152

The away team, down to seven men, is desperately holding on to a draw when the home side score what has to be the winner. As soon as play restarts, you are shocked to see the away captain violently elbow an opponent. It's a clear attempt to get himself sent off and for you to abandon the game. What do you do?

Late in a game, a defender, whose side are 4-0 up, instinctively sticks out a hand to stop a shot flying into the net. Realising it's a sending off offence, he smashes the dropping ball into the net with his foot. What action do you take?

The ball suddenly breaks upfield and a striker races after it totally unchallenged. As he runs over the halfway line a defender manages to catch up and tugs his shoulder, bringing him down. The striker only had the keeper to beat, but was 40 yards from goal. What do you do?

A cup tie has gone to penalties. At 5-4 the next player starts his run up. Halfway to the ball he slows, hoping the keeper will commit himself, but the keeper stands still. The taker continues to hesitate and on reaching the ball, stops and without having touched it, turns around and says he needs to start again. What do you do?

157 Deep into stoppage time, a defender on a yellow card is deliberately time wasting while being subbed. Even after you warn him, he still dawdles, provoking uproar from the players and fans of the opposing team. What do you do?

159 A keeper saves a weak penalty kick, prompting the defender who gave it away to dash over and embrace him. As he does so, his hand clearly touches the ball, which is still clutched by the goalkeeper. The opposing team howl for a retake. What now?

158 You allow a free kick to be taken quickly, but a defender stands in front of the ball to stop play. The angry kick-taker responds by kicking the ball at him, then volleying the rebound into the net. Is it a goal?

After a sudden pre-match blizzard, the pitch is playable but covered with snow. The groundsman repaints the lines, but you notice that while most of them are black, some are red. He says he ran out of black paint. Can the game go ahead?

160

161

A time-wasting keeper is furious after you award an indirect free kick against him for holding the ball for longer than six seconds. He drops the ball, puts his foot on it, and starts shouting at you. But as he does so, an opponent reacts by toe-poking the ball from under the keeper's boot into the net. What now?

At half time you check your Twitter feed and notice a player you booked in the first half has just tweeted a grossly offensive message about you to his followers. How do you react?

162

As a striker lines up to take a shot, you are baffled to see the nearest defender pull out of the tackle. Instead, screaming for play to stop, he bends down and picks up a pair of scissors that must have fallen out of the physio's bag earlier. What now?

164

163

A player whose team have already had four red cards commits a second yellow card offence, but there is a chance to play advantage as the opposition are in on goal. What do you do?

A substitute warming up behind the team's goal sees his keeper being chipped – so instinctively races onto the pitch and tips the ball over the bar, preventing a certain goal. What action do you take?

165

A striker is flagged offside as he races into the area. In his frustration he ignores your whistle and dribbles past the keeper, but the keeper wanting to get on with the game, trips him over with an excessive force and picks up the ball. What now?

166

167

A keeper makes a stunning last-minute penalty save, tipping the ball on to the post, as a defender boots it upfield the keeper celebrates wildly in front of the fans waving his shirt in the air. He has already been booked. Do you intervene?

Just as the away team's star striker takes a vital late penalty, the stadium's PA blares out MISS YOU by the Rolling Stones. The player scuffs his kick over the bar. There's uproar. Do you allow him to retake it?

168

In a crowded penalty area, a flamboyant forward attempts an overhead kick. But a defender puts two arms around him and prevents him from getting airborne. Had the striker been able to complete the kick, you would have penalised him for dangerous play. What now?

169

170

A keeper catches a corner but runs to you shouting that he's seen and heard people making monkey chants in the crowd. In his haste, he carries the ball out of the area. What do you do?

A defender inside the area intentionally stops a goal-bound shot with his shoulder. The ball drops and clearly strikes his arm on the way to the ground. Is it a penalty?

171

A three-way clash in the penalty area leaves a striker and a defender injured. You show the keeper who caused it a red card and award a penalty. The keeper's manager then tells you he wants the injured defender to go in goal after he has received treatment. Do you allow it?

172

173

You are surprised to see a penalty-taker spit on the ball like a cricketer before placing it on the spot. He says it's for luck; the keeper says it's disgusting and demands that you change the ball. What do you do?

A striker, who is already on a yellow card, scores his 100th goal for his club. To celebrate he sprints over to his bench, collects a special spare shirt with the number 100 on the back, and pulls it on over his normal top. What do you do?

174

In the middle of a match, a player's mobile phone rings in his pocket. Standing in the centre circle, he takes it out and starts talking on it as play goes on around him. Do you intervene?

175

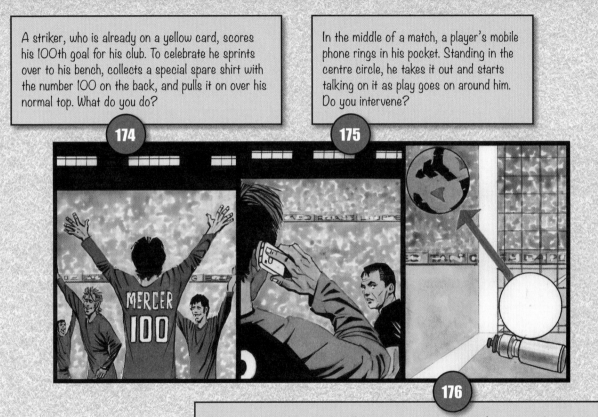

176

A shot rebounds downwards off the bar, hits the goalkeeper's water bottle, and deflects back into play. The goal-line sensor does not register it crossing the line and you are unsure. The attacking team are furious. What now?

177 Without using directly abusive language, during a break in play, a striker goads an opponent about rumours over his sexuality and makes a gesture towards him. What do you do?

179 A goal is scored right at the start of the second half. You suspect it was offside, but when you look to your colleague for guidance, you realise that both assistants are mistakenly operating in the other half of the pitch. What now?

178 As two players brawl on the edge of the area, the keeper races out to try and pull them apart. But as he does so – and before you have had a chance to stop play – a striker takes advantage and chips the ball into the unguarded net. Goal or no goal?

Just before the start of a sweltering World Cup match, you notice one side have no subs on their bench. The manager explains he is keeping them in the air-conditioned dressing room watching the game on television and he'll call them when he needs them. Do you intervene?

180

The away team's keeper is facing his old club, which he left in controversial circumstances the previous summer. The home crowd are on his case from the start, and in the second half you notice him shouting at the home fans behind his goal. A senior steward tells you the keeper racially abused a fan in the front row. The keeper denies it. What do you do?

182

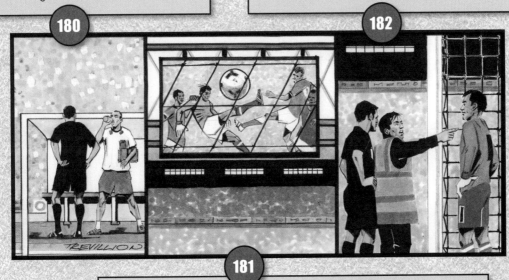

181

As you award a goal, your assistant flags and tells you the keeper was fouled. You disagree but, just as you prepare to restart, you see a replay of the incident on the big screen. The foul is obvious. What now?

In a cup tie, both teams have red home shirts and blue away shirts. They tell you they have done a deal whereby one team will wear their home shirts in the first half and the other team will wear their home shirts in the second half. Do you let them do this?

183

You arrive for a game at a multisport stadium and find rugby pitch markings are still visible in white, while the football lines have been painted on top in blue. What action do you take?

185

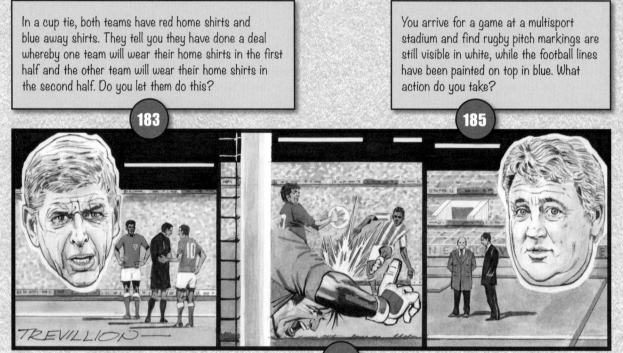

TREVILLION

184

The keeper blocks a shot with a scorpion kick, but lands badly, screams and immediately signals he is injured. A striker latches on to the rebound and shoots at the unguarded goal. But a defender catches the ball, pointing at the prostrate keeper. What do you do?

Two players from the same team collide with each other. Both need treatment, although the injuries are not serious. The ball stays in play. Do you intervene?

186

A fashion-conscious winger is wearing one blue and one white boot, paired with matching official club socks of different colours. The opposition defenders complain it gives him an advantage. What now?

187

188

Behind at half time, the away team make three substitutions, and within 15 minutes of the start of the second half have made a stunning comeback goal. But soon after, you realise to your horror that they actually made four changes – one of them the identical twin of one of the starting lineup. What now?

Ten minutes after kick off, a defender on the goal line instinctively sticks out a hand to block a goal-bound shot. But before you blow, keen to avoid such an early red card, he quickly knocks the ball into his own net. What do you do?

190

189

In searing heat, a tired defence pushes out. But one of the defenders is too exhausted to sprint, so instead he steps out of play, putting an attacker offside. What now?

191

Five minutes into a game, one of the captains complains that his side are having trouble distinguishing between their strip and that of their opponents. Both have orange sleeves. Do you order one side to change tops, abandon the match, or play on?

In sweltering heat, the sprinklers are turned on at half time but cover only one half of the pitch. It means the home side will have a double advantage – their attackers playing on a fast surface, and their defenders operating on a slow one. The visitors are outraged. What now?

192

The home side's captain is tired and wants to come off. So when he sees his manager using his final change to replace someone else, he's furious. He tells his colleague to stay on the pitch and walks off himself, shaking hands with the sub as he goes. There's uproar. What now?

194

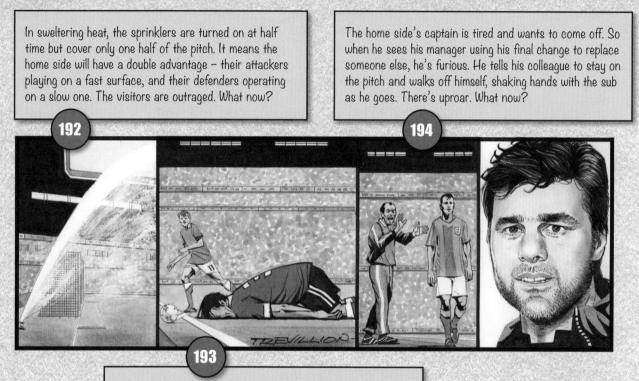

193

In the 90th minute, a pacey young winger nutmegs a veteran defender, who groans and collapses, apparently unconscious. Fearing for his health, the winger stops running towards goal and kicks the ball out, only for the defender to make a miraculous recovery. You suspect foul play. What do you do?

During stoppage time of a stormy game, you award a hotly disputed penalty, your fourth of the match. The taker, whose side are 2-1 up, decides to stage a protest to make you look stupid, instead of taking a shot, he just taps the ball forward an inch then calls on you to blow for full time. What now?

195

As the home side cling on to a tense one-goal lead, you notice that the ball boys keep fumbling spare balls onto the pitch, wasting time. An away player starts shouting at them. What action do you take?

197

TREVILLION

196

A home-team striker, playing against his old club for the first time, has taken sustained abuse from the visiting fans. When he scores, he races over to them and cups his ears. The fans react in fury, pelting him with plastic bottles. What do you do?

The away team's captain complains that the home keeper is hard to see clearly because his shirt blends in with the colours of the goal nets. What action do you take?

198

When the ball is cleared off the line at the end of stoppage time in the 95th minute, you blow for full time. But after your third peep, your wristband buzzes to indicate that the ball had crossed the line. Goal or no goal?

200

199

Before the game you're bemused by an unusual request from the away team's manager. He says that his team are set piece specialists, so he does not want you to play advantage when his players are fouled. He wants you to award free kicks instead. How do you respond?

A manager has told his assistant to stand on the edge of their technical area and film the away side's famously aggressive striker in case of any incidents. The away manager complains. What do you do?

201

You spot a substitute injecting himself while waiting to come on. Given the player's reputation, you think he could be using a banned substance, but the player and the physio deny it. What now?

203

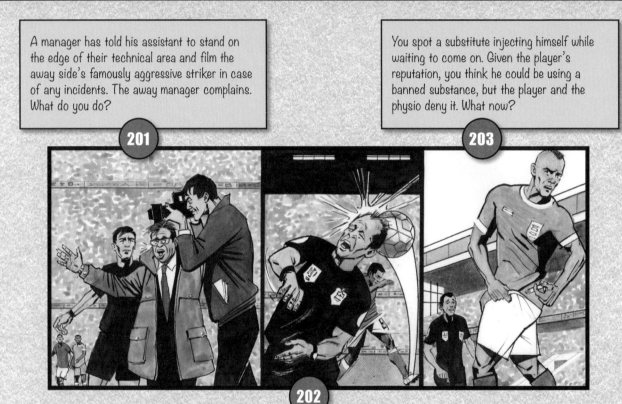

202

You are briefly knocked out by a shot. When you come to, you see one of your assistants has awarded a goal and the players are celebrating. How do you respond?

A striker who is through on goal is pulled down by a chasing defender, so you instantly pull out your red card and dismiss him. But as he walks off, you spot your assistant waving his flag. He tells you the striker was offside. What now?

204

A striker has a shoulder injury, but with all the subs used and his side hanging on to a one-goal lead, he and his manager want him to play in defence for the final six minutes. You think he is seriously injured. Do you force him to leave the field and bring his side down to ten men?

206

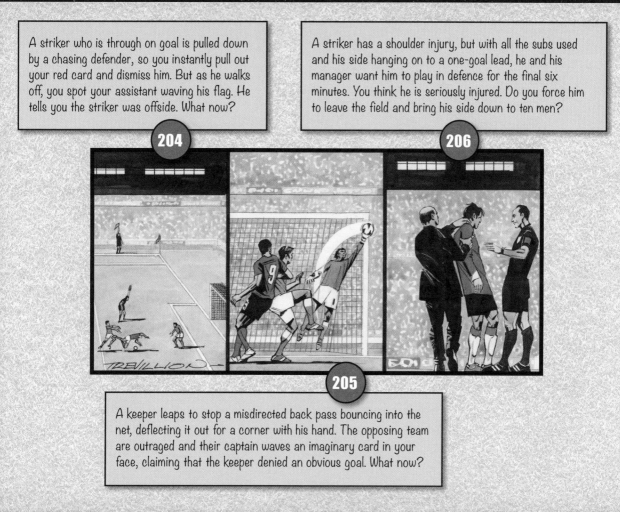

205

A keeper leaps to stop a misdirected back pass bouncing into the net, deflecting it out for a corner with his hand. The opposing team are outraged and their captain waves an imaginary card in your face, claiming that the keeper denied an obvious goal. What now?

A player clean through on goal is brought down by the last defender outside the penalty area. You play advantage because the ball has run to another attacker, but as this player races into the area, the keeper brings him down without challenging for the ball. What now?

207

In a Champions League tie, a winger racing in from the corner spots the additional assistant standing on the goal line, so plays the ball off his leg to get past a defender. The ball hasn't left the pitch. What do you do?

209

208

Before a penalty shoot-out, the keeper wants to change his shirt in order to wear his lucky colour, which is distinctive. Do you let him?

Three minutes before half time during a bleak midwinter match, the floodlights fail. The stadium manager says it will take ten minutes to fix them, and suggests you blow for half time now. What do you do?

210

It's 1–1 in added time of a cup tie. One of the goalkeepers, who has been heroic throughout, catches a easy ball, then bizarrely fumbles it into his own net before collapsing. After treatment, he says he has no memory of what happened and the medics say he had some sort of seizure. Do you award the goal?

212

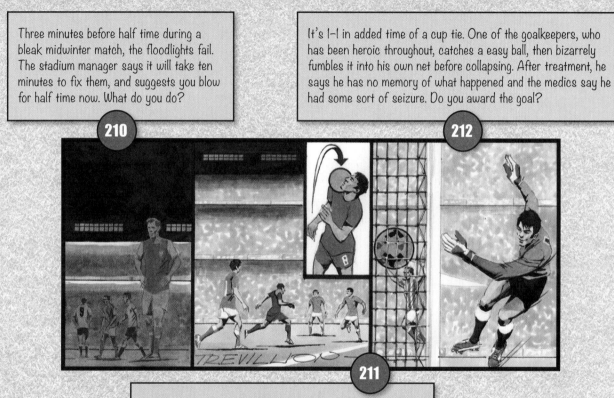

211

A maverick winger known for his juggling skills deftly flicks the ball up and balances it between his jaw and shoulder. He then manages to run 30 yards before letting it drop and volleying it into the net. Goal or no goal?

A goalkeeper takes a short goal kick towards a defender. The defender, spotting a striker bearing down on him, reacts by dashing inside the box and passing the ball back to the keeper before it leaves the area. What do you do?

213

A striker deliberately plays the ball off your leg. It deflects to a teammate, who shoots and scores. Goal or no goal?

215

214

An enraged defender swings a punch at a striker. The striker, who also happens to be a martial arts expert, blocks the punch before it connects and twists the defender's arm sharply behind his back. How many red cards do you show?

An unconventional coach keeps handing his players energy bars during breaks in play. Your assistant complains about having to run through the wrappers littering the touchline. Do you intervene?

216

A player in an offside position receives the ball directly from a throw-in and races clear. But as he does so, your assistant flags and you stop the game, assuming he has spotted a foul. Then you realise he was mistakenly flagging for offside. What do you do?

217

218

In an end of season thriller, the home team need a draw to stay up and the away team need to win to claim the title. In the closing minutes with the score at 1-1, an away fan runs on and knocks out the home keeper. The home side have used all their subs, and refuse to continue with an outfield player in goal. What now?

In wet conditions a striker skids as he leaps to head a corner. To avoid injury, he grabs the post and swings around it. As he does so, the ball hits him and goes in. Goal or no goal?

219

A player on a yellow card suddenly runs off the pitch and down the tunnel without explanation. He reappears two minutes later in the technical area, desperate to get back on. You decide to ignore him until there is a stoppage in play, but he runs back on anyway. What now?

220

221

A quick-thinking young defender stops a goal-bound shot by stretching his shirt out to block the ball. It drops at his feet and he boots it clear. Do you intervene?

In hot conditions during a pre-season tournament, the teams are level and exhausted after 90 minutes. For safety reasons, both managers ask you to agree to go straight to a penalty shoot-out. Do you let them?

223

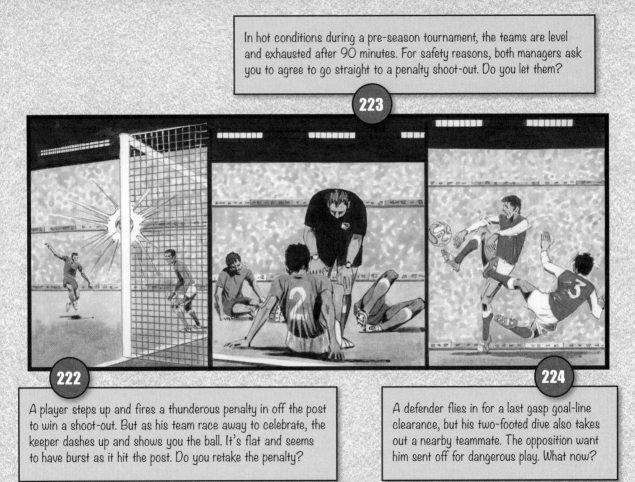

222

A player steps up and fires a thunderous penalty in off the post to win a shoot-out. But as his team race away to celebrate, the keeper dashes up and shows you the ball. It's flat and seems to have burst as it hit the post. Do you retake the penalty?

224

A defender flies in for a last gasp goal-line clearance, but his two-footed dive also takes out a nearby teammate. The opposition want him sent off for dangerous play. What now?

Just after the start of a penalty shoot-out, you're surprised to see the away side's chairman storming over to you waving a copy of the competition rulebook. He says you've overlooked the away goals rule, and his side has already won. To your horror, you realise he's right. What now?

225

With his championship team 7–0 up in a home cup-tie against a non-league side, the bored keeper starts listening to music via earphones concealed in his cap. Do you intervene?

227

226

Early in a game you spot a player is not wearing shin pads, so you order him off to put some on. But, after he returns and scores, you notice he has actually shoved two match-day programmes down his socks. He says he doesn't like the feel of plastic pads. What do you do?

A mascot is parading along the touchline during play. He is wearing the club colours and is distracting you and your assistants. Can you send a mascot to the stands?

228

The home team scores a stunning goal that you agree is valid. But the away players surround you pointing downfield to where they claim their striker was 'nutted' before the goal was scored. You turn and see two players – one from each team – writhing in pain. What now?

230

229

A keeper comes up for a late corner kick in a junior game played on a smaller pitch. But his opposite number clears the corner with a powerful punch. The ball flies upfield and bounces into the unguarded goal. Is it a goal?

A team is trying to run down the clock with a new tactic. Their defenders repeatedly block goal kicks from leaving the penalty area, meaning they have to be retaken. Can you intervene?

231

A player scores a late winner and he and his twin take off their shirts in celebration. But a confrontation with an opposing player ensues, and one twin punches him. You've no idea which one, and they blame each other. What now?

232

233

After seeing his penalty brilliantly saved in a shoot-out a striker sportingly hugs the keeper to congratulate him. But as he does so, the ball spins back over the line. Goal, retake or foul?

A player scores on the rebound from a saved penalty. The opposition are furious, they say the scorer, who had been off the field for treatment, came back on without your permission during the row that followed your penalty award. What now?

234

A team, already down to eight players due to red cards and injuries, manages to hang on to a draw and take their cup semi-final to a penalty shoot-out. But before it starts, two of their star players get into a heated row over who takes the first kick and they start trading punches. What action do you take?

235

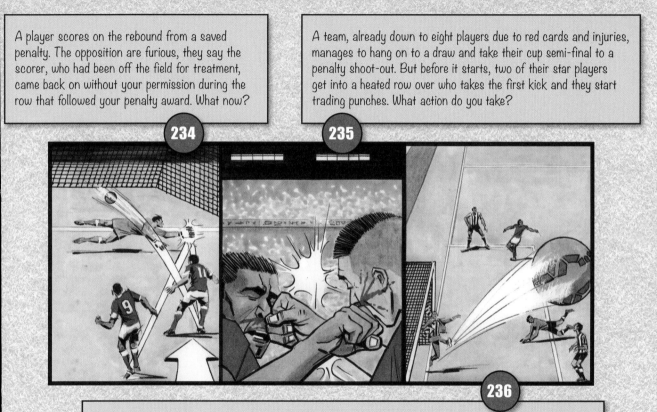

236

It's the final minutes of a tense derby locked at 0–0. The away side's striker beats the keeper only to see his shot booted off the line by a teenage pitch invader. The furious striker pushes the boy to the floor, but the home captain picks him up and parades him on his shoulders as a hero. It's chaos. What do you do?

In a penalty shoot-out, the keeper parries a shot but the ball spins back towards goal. The taker reacts by racing after it and using his body to block the keeper from reaching it and protect the ball as it crosses the line. Goal or no goal?

237

A player known for his trademark hairstyle leaps to head a looping cross and for a second appears to trap the ball with his hair. With defenders briefly unable to make a legal challenge, he lets the ball drop and smashes it into the net. What now?

238

239

A winger wildly scuffs a cross, which balloons up and over the area. His momentum takes him off the pitch, and he sprints behind the goal to retrieve the ball before it goes out for a throw. He crosses the ball again and it is headed in. What do you do?

A striker injures his wrist during a game but, as his team are a goal down and have used their subs, the physio straps it up and he goes back on. Awaiting a corner, a defender gives the striker's injured wrist a gentle tap and he collapses in agony. His teammates demand a penalty. The defender claims he is play-acting. What's your decision?

240

The home keeper is wearing no gloves and a short-sleeved jersey, and his teammates are also in short sleeves. At half time you are informed that television replays have shown that a home defender – not the goalkeeper – has twice punched the ball away in the crowded penalty area. What now?

241

242

Every player is up, including the attacking side's goalkeeper, for a last-minute corner. The ball is cleared down to the other end and a defender and forward race for it, well ahead of the chasing pack. They both miss it but their momentum takes them behind the goal line. The forward is quicker to turn and is about to re-enter the pitch when the defender grabs his ankle to stop him. What action do you take?

A striker, who has been repeatedly fouled, brandishes an imaginary card following the latest incident, so you book him. But as the game goes on and the fouls continue, he pointedly keeps count, reminding you of the running tally. What do you do?

243

In a rain-soaked junior game, a long ball reaches the centre forward who is onside, racing towards goal. But the chasing defender suddenly slips, falls forward, and accidentally pulls the striker down. What action do you take?

244

245

At the end of a relegation decider, in which the home side avoided the drop via a hotly contested penalty, the home captain offers to swap shirts on the way to the tunnel. It's your final match before retirement. What is your response?

You've awarded a very late penalty and have to extend stoppage time so it can be taken. But the identified kick-taker doesn't take the shot. Instead a teammate rushes in and slots it home. The furious keeper says it's an illegal move, then insists you can't give a retake because time has now run out. What do you do?

246

A manager, who has been complaining in the press about shirt-pulling has secretly had his players' shirts fitted with Velcro seams. Soon after kick-off, you're shocked to see a goalmouth melée result in three defenders each holding pieces of shirt, while three shirtless attackers scream for a penalty. What now?

247

248

It's a late corner kick to the away side. But the home fans won't give the ball back. You signal for the kick to be taken with a replacement ball. But as you do so, a fan throws the original ball back onto the pitch. The angry corner-taker reacts by booting the replacement ball into the crowd behind the goal, then takes a quick corner with the original ball. Do you intervene?

In the closing seconds of the Women's World Cup final a corner is whipped in. You see the ball strike an arm, but you can't see who the arm belonged to. As you hesitate, the ball drops to a striker, who thrashes it into the net. Your assistant shrugs. What now?

249

A striker, clean through on goal, is sent flying, fouled by the two chasing defenders and the outrushing keeper simultaneously. What do you do?

251

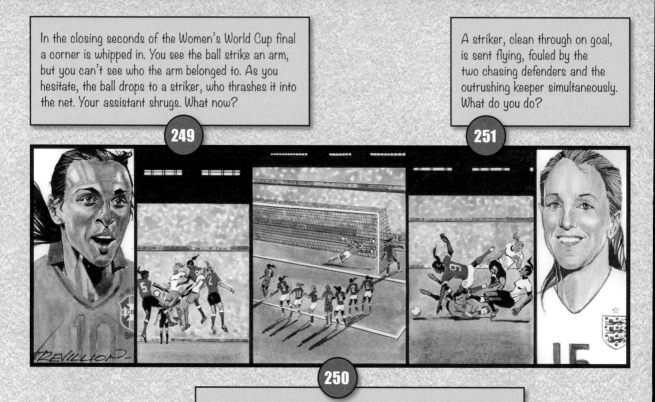

250

As a direct free kick is fired into the box, the defenders move back to catch an attacker offside. But the attacker, standing by the goal line, deliberately steps back off the pitch. The ball sails into the net just where she was standing. Goal or no goal?

252
A player is hurt in a goalmouth scramble. But with no subs left and his team down to ten men already, he tells you he wants to stay on the pitch for the final ten minutes. He says he will stand still inside the opponent's penalty area. Do you let him?

253
A defender in the wall jumps and turns as a direct free kick is blasted at goal. The ball cannons against the top of his arm and deflects to safety behind the goal line. The attackers scream for a penalty. What is your decision?

254
A keeper prepares to take a free kick from just outside his own penalty area. He places the ball, then quickly steps beyond it to shout instructions to a teammate. But as he steps back again, he accidentally backheels the ball into his own goal. How do you restart?

255

A star striker is sent flying in the penalty area. He receives treatment on the field, then prepares to take the crucial penalty, but opponents insist he has to leave the field before play restarts. Are they right?

256

During a crucial game, the home side's captain vomits on the pitch. He is clearly ill but refuses to be substituted and his manager is also determined to keep him on. Do you insist on a substitution?

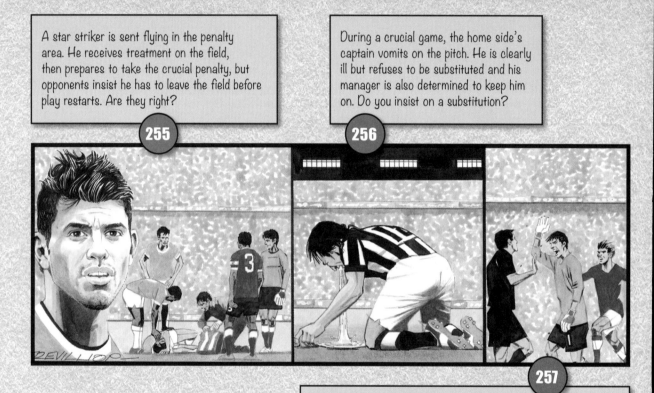

257

A striker tries to use his hand to slip the ball into the net. As you blow the whistle, the keeper races towards you, screaming for you to send off the striker. Both players are already on a yellow card. What now?

In the dying seconds of a game, your assistant thinks he has seen you blowing for full time and stoops to pick up the ball, which had bounced in front of him. Realising his error, he drops it again, allowing a nearby striker to shoot and score. What now?

258

A fierce wind blows the home manager's notes onto the pitch and they land next to an away player. The player, who had been booked ten minutes earlier, reacts by tearing up the notes and laughingly throwing the pieces into the air. What do you do?

259

260

Two players try a clever penalty. One taps the ball forward while the other runs forward from outside the penalty area. But before the second player can reach the ball, a defender brings him down. But the ball runs free and another attacker smacks it into the net. What now?

Two overseas players are in a heated argument, shouting in a mix of English and their own language. You only understand the English words and hear one of them replying, 'Well you are a xxxxx too'. It's a clear racial insult. What do you do?

261

Instead of blowing for a foul, you play advantage. The fouled player passes to a teammate, but the teammate reacts by picking up the ball and rolling it back towards you, ready for a free kick. He is already on a yellow and the opposing team scream for a red. What happens next?

263

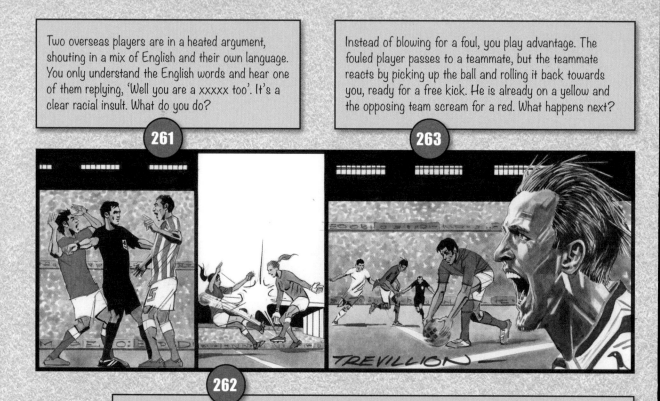

262

A striker and a keeper sprint towards each other for a loose ball bouncing into the penalty area. At the last minute the striker decides to duck out of the challenge and stops dead, but the keeper's momentum makes a collision inevitable. The keeper clears the ball, then sends the striker flying. What now?

You play advantage after a winger is the victim of a reckless challenge only to see him hit by another reckless tackle from the same defender. As the ball rolls out for a corner, the attacking team, famous for their corner routines, demand the right to take the corner, rather than a free kick. What do you do?

264

The home team make their final substitution with five minutes left. But as the subbed player leaves, the replacement refuses to come on, still angry about having been dropped to the bench. So the manager tells you he is cancelling the change and sending the subbed player back on. Do you let him?

266

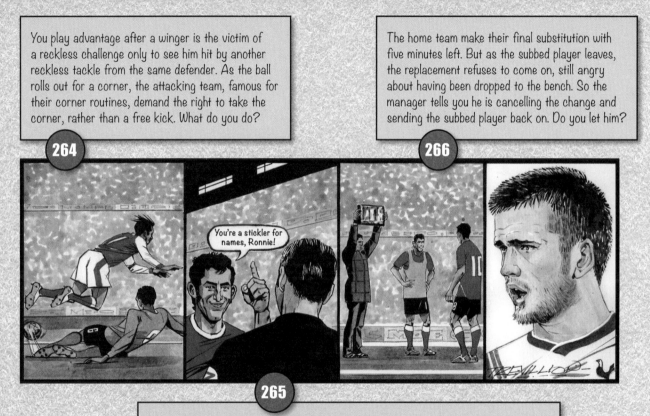

265

When you book the home captain and ask him to confirm his name he just smirks and says, 'You know who I am.' When you insist he relents, but then spends the rest of the game sarcastically using your first name at every encounter. How do you react?

A striker struggles to reach a cross which has been whipped low and hard into the goal area, so he deliberately takes a swing at a pile of snow in his path. He manages to kick enough of it to divert the cross into the net without making direct contact with the ball. Goal or no goal?

A new signing coming on as a sub for his debut, has his nickname 'Rambo' on the back of his shirt instead of his real name. Do you intervene?

267

269

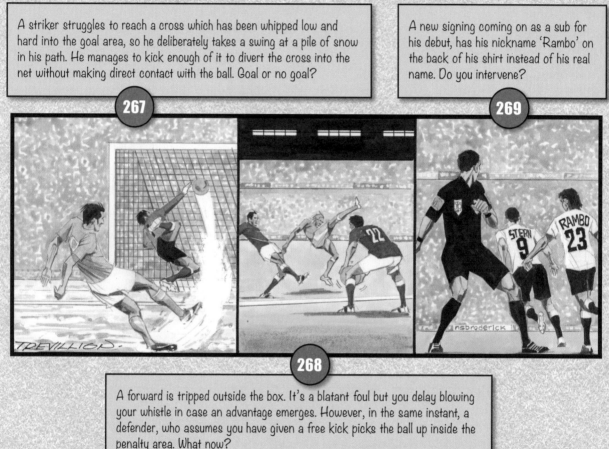

268

A forward is tripped outside the box. It's a blatant foul but you delay blowing your whistle in case an advantage emerges. However, in the same instant, a defender, who assumes you have given a free kick picks the ball up inside the penalty area. What now?

The away captain, outraged by your decisions, reacts to going 3–0 down at half time by dribbling the ball back to his own goal after the second-half kick off, stopping it on the line, and offering you the chance to boot it into the net. The other players watch open mouthed. Do you stop play?

270

The home side score a vital late goal in a final-day relegation decider, prompting a minor pitch invasion. When the fans are cleared, you discover one of them has cut away a piece of one of the goal nets as a souvenir. There is no spare net and there are two minutes of added time still to play. What now?

271

272

While a player is receiving treatment on the pitch, a teammate takes some freeze spray from the physio's bag and sprays his own painful ankle. Do you make him leave the pitch before re-starting?

A keeper wildly slices a goal kick in your direction. Without thinking, you instinctively knock the ball back to the keeper, who picks it up before a nearby striker can reach it. You've denied a goal-scoring opportunity. What do you do?

273

All three of the home side's goals have come via enormous punts upfield by the keeper. But when you stop play after he goes down injured, you notice his kicking boot has a metal toecap. What now?

274

275

During a European cup tie, some of the home crowd shout racial abuse at the away team players. The chanting is clear, but the players being targeted and their captain urge you not to abandon the game because they are winning 3–0. What now?

You spot a player shouting at your assistant, so you show him a yellow card. Later in the game the pair clash again, but nearby opponents say your colleague started it. What now?

276

During a penalty shoot-out the home captain comes over to complain that the away keeper has put on unusually large boots, apparently with the heels padded out with newspaper, meaning he can stand ahead of the goal line with his heels still touching it. Do you intervene?

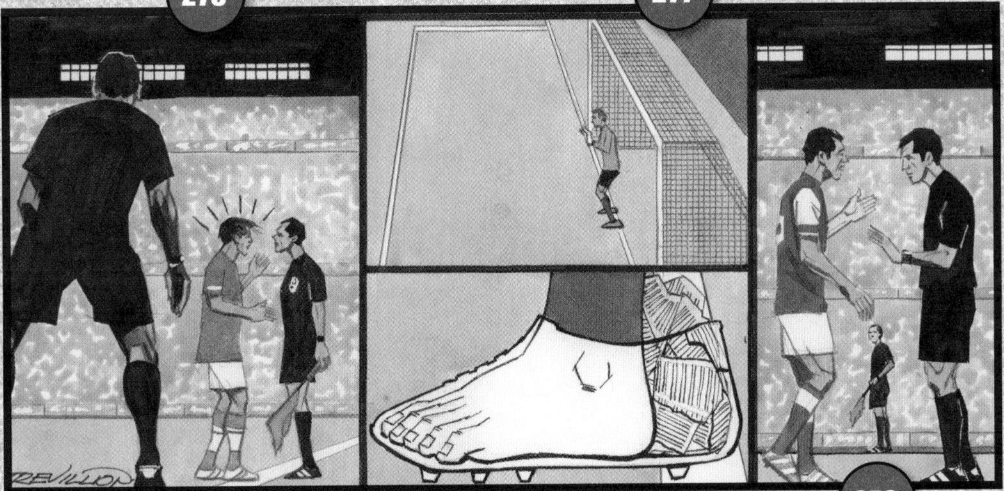

277

278

Just before kick off a player approaches you. He says he went to school with one of your assistants and they have been feuding for years. He says the assistant always picks on him and wants him replaced. What now?

A player slips on the sodden pitch as he takes a vital late penalty and ends up kicking the ground just behind the ball. The scoop of mud propels the ball forward. As the delighted keeper easily picks up the ball, the attacking side demand a retake. What now?

In a lower league game, the players have booted all the available match balls out of the ground. The home team's kit man suggests using a spare size 4 ball to complete the final ten minutes, and both teams agree. What's your decision?

279

281

280

The floodlights fail in an evening game halfway through a penalty shoot-out. When the stadium manager reveals the fault cannot be fixed, both managers ask permission to complete the shoot-out in the failing light rather than risk having the whole game replayed. What do you do?

As a penalty taker strikes the ball he grunts loudly. The distracted keeper is outraged and makes no attempt to save the shot. He demands a retake. What do you do?

282

Players and officials assemble for a Sunday-league game only to find an artificial cricket strip across the goal area. Both teams are happy to play. What do you do?

283

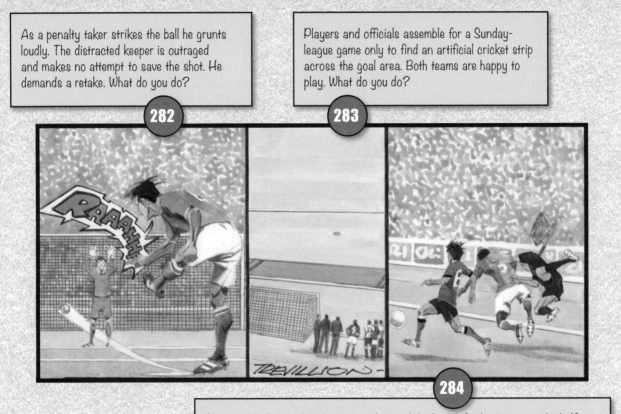

284

Chasing a ball over the top, an attacker and the last defender race over the halfway line on the wing. Your assistant turns so he can sprint after them but slips and falls, knocking over the defender. The attacker has a clear run on goal. What now?

As you consult your assistant over an off-the-ball incident, the players crowd around trying to hear. As you ask them to back off, you're shocked to hear your assistant shouting at them, using foul and aggressive language. What now?

285

A winger jinks past the diving keeper to slot the ball into an unguarded net but is sent flying by a chasing defender, who has tripped over his own keeper. It's a clear accident. What now?

286

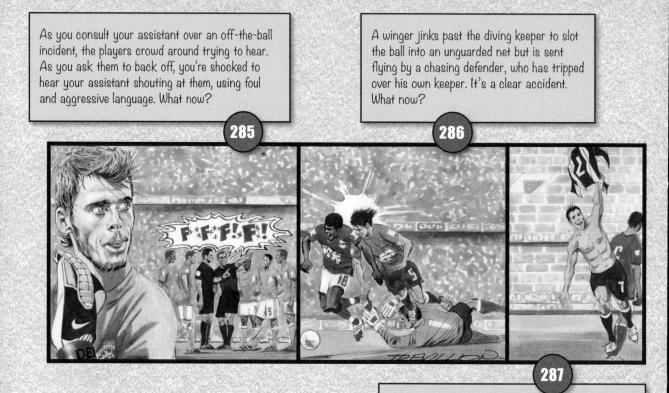

287

Due to crowd violence, the match you are refereeing is being played behind closed doors. A striker, who is already on a yellow card, scores and rips his shirt off in celebration. Do you intervene?

A keeper races out and knocks the ball out of play for a throw. He then quickly picks up the ball and, before releasing it to the opposition, carries it with him as he runs back into his penalty area. Do you intervene?

288

Before a match you find the goalposts at both ends have been painted in the sponsor's colours. The crowd are arriving, do you let the game go ahead?

289

290

A defender standing on his goal line instinctively catches a goal-bound shot. You blow your whistle, but then notice, to your dismay, that the ball is a different colour and a different brand to those you inspected before the start of the game. It's a size 4 ball and you have been playing with it for at least ten minutes. What now?

A midfielder deliberately plays a pass off an opponent who is lying injured, deflecting the ball into the path of a striker who would otherwise have been offside. What do you do?

291

A defender traps a long, hoofed clearance inside his empty penalty area, and then, leaving the ball stationary, trots up field. The keeper walks over and picks the ball up. Back pass or no back pass?

292

293

Before taking a free kick on the edge of the area, a striker moves the ball back a yard, to give him a better angle. The wall reacts by moving forward a yard and over your foam line. What now?

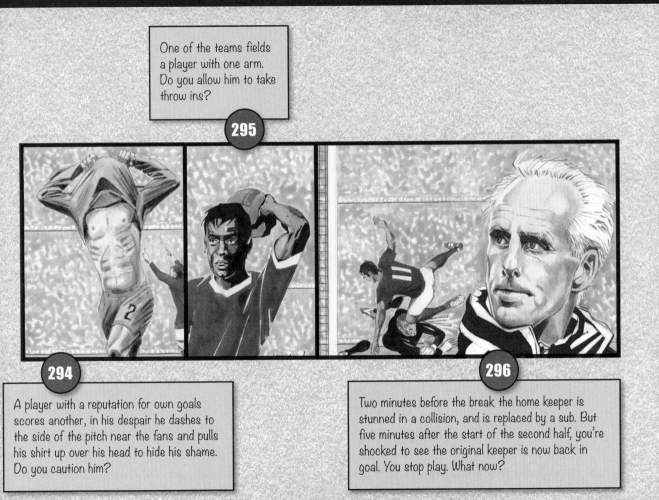

295 One of the teams fields a player with one arm. Do you allow him to take throw ins?

294 A player with a reputation for own goals scores another, in his despair he dashes to the side of the pitch near the fans and pulls his shirt up over his head to hide his shame. Do you caution him?

296 Two minutes before the break the home keeper is stunned in a collision, and is replaced by a sub. But five minutes after the start of the second half, you're shocked to see the original keeper is now back in goal. You stop play. What now?

As play continues after you have made a decision that has annoyed the home crowd, a fan runs onto the pitch in an apparent attempt to attack you. But before he reaches you, a player steps in and violently sends him flying, saving you from assault. What now?

297

In stormy weather with a striker challenging him, a keeper dives to smother the ball on the edge of his penalty area. He grabs it, only for his momentum to send him into a puddle, and outside the area. Do you punish him, or abandon the game?

298

TREVILLON

299

As a defender makes a last-ditch tackle, he catches his studs in the turf and badly breaks his leg. The striker evades him and does not notice the injury, unlike the keeper, who raises his hands and rushes out to help his teammate. The striker scores. Goal or no goal?

300

In the closing minutes of a frantic, but goalless, end-to-end derby, both teams make a number of quick substitutions. In the 89th minute the keeper drops a corner kick and a goal is scored. You then notice to your horror that the team now leading has 12 players. What action do you take?

THE ANSWERS

Page 16

1 What a mess. Your colleague is guilty of both a poor original decision, and some poor positioning here. The flag should not be hovering over the line like this when play is live, but you have no reason to stop play, so the onside player can continue his run on goal. The officials and their flags are considered part of the field of play.

2 Although this incident ocurred after the final whistle, you can still issue sanctions. You may sympathise with the defender's reaction, but you have to stick to the laws. Show him a straight red card for violent conduct – the striker was struck in the face – and show the striker a second yellow card, followed by a red, for unsporting behaviour.

Page 17 Roy Hodgson

3 Under the old interpretation of the offside law, your assistant would have flagged the moment the ball was played towards the striker. But these days an offside offence is not committed until the player involved becomes active. Therefore, as play was still live, the defender is guilty of a straightforward deliberate handball. Award a penalty and show a yellow card. The card is not red because, had the ball reached the striker, he would then have been flagged, so there was no goal-scoring opportunity.

4 The ball is in contact with the defender's hand inside the penalty area while play is live, and the action was deliberate, so show him a yellow card and award a penalty. The fact that the offence started outside the box is irrelevant.

5 Delay the corner and call both players over to you. Show each a yellow card unless the defender pushed the striker in the face, in which case he should receive a red card. As play was not live, no penalty should be given. Restart with a corner.

Page 18

6 The foam line is there as only a visual guide – the final call on whether the players also moved forward as well as sideways is yours. If they did not move forward before the ball was kicked, play on. If you believe they did, award a retake. The foam line is a useful introduction but does does not always reduce controversy.

7 Send the defender off – a second yellow, then a red. He clearly attempted to trip the attacker with a reckless challenge. Restart the game with a penalty for the offence. It doesn't matter that no contact was made. In this situation, you cannot also punish the attacker for simulation, because if he had not dived out of the way, he could have been seriously hurt.

8 There is no offence. The player has re-joined the game with your permission – albeit briefly. So as long as you are sure that the ball was fully out of play before he caught it, the player is within his rights to step back, catch the ball, and take the throw.

Page 19

9 Whether the star player's teammate is being unusually honest or is just trying to save the star from dismissal is irrelevant. Either way, you have to stick with your judgement, and not base your decisions on what players tell you. Send off the star for a second yellow card offence and, if you think the teammate was deliberately lying to you, show him a yellow card too.

10 No goal. You should really have blown the whistle before the ball rolled into the goal. As it is, restart with a dropped ball on the goal area line parallel to the goal line, nearest to where the ball entered the net. It's worth noting that, if the mud had been flicked or thrown deliberately, you would have to show a red card, and restart with a direct free kick to the defending team.

11 Show the injured substitute a yellow card for entering the field of play without permission. The substitution had not been completed because the original player had not left the pitch. Therefore you must allow the manager to cancel the change and use another sub instead.

Page 20 Steph Houghton

12 You really have to intervene here. At the next stoppage, ask the mascot to remove his head so you can see who is inside. If it is the banned manager, order him to leave the stadium and report what has happened to the authorities. If not, instruct the mascot to cool down, and stay away from the pitch perimeter.

13 It depends how he has dropped on the ball. If he has used his hands, penalise him for handling the back pass by awarding an indirect free kick – it doesn't matter that he went on a dribble first. But if he has just used his body to drop on the ball and shield it from an opponent, you need to watch what happens next. If he gets up and clears the ball without handling it and without the opponent challenging him, play on. But if an opponent tries to kick the ball from under him, you have to stop the game. In that situation, the keeper has created a dangerous situation (a danger to himself). Penalise him for dangerous play with an indirect free kick.

14 You need to stop play and rule that the corner be re-taken. The flag post needs to be in the correct position when the ball is kicked.

Page 21 Sean Dyche

15 You can only base a decision on what you or your assistants heard, so however much their complaint makes sense, if you did not hear the shout, you cannot take action. But if you did hear it, disallow the goal, book the striker for unsporting behaviour, and restart with an indirect free kick to the defending team.

16 The player who was fouled has taken a real risk here, but you should still punish the first offence. However, before you restart with a free kick, remind the player to play to the whistle.

17 There are three offences here, and you need to deal with all of them. Stop play and show the two defenders a yellow card each for holding. Then show the attacker who shoved his marker in the face a red card for violent conduct. Now you have the option of restarting with a dropped ball from where it was when you blew the whistle. However, it is better to punish one of the offences more severely. So if you decide the defenders' actions were the most serious, award a penalty. If, as is more likely, you think the shove in the face was the worse offence, it's a direct free kick to the defending team.

Page 22 Per Mertesacker

18 Here's a situation where common sense must prevail. According to the rules, since the signal for the corner was given, there was no offence and it's a valid goal, but in reality you need to acknowledge your mistake. You were wrong to signal for the kick before the sub was in place, so disallow the goal and order the corner to be taken again. And learn your lesson: this is a basic refereeing mistake.

19 You are not supposed to view video footage but this is a hugely serious situation, so you should make an exception and act on it. First, the video clearly shows that, for whatever reason, your assistant saw the offence and chose not to inform you, so you relieve him of his duties. Tell him he will be reported and arrange for another qualified person, if available, to take over. Secondly, inform both managers that you will be reporting the incident in full. And thirdly, tell the home manager that grabbing you is unacceptable, and you are excluding him from the technical area for the remainder of the match. A nightmare scenario.

20 Play on. It was clearly not a deliberate pass to the keeper, so there's no offence. Any attacking player who appeals for a back pass is being opportunistic.

Page 23

21 Officials use the 'PIG' system to judge offside – namely, did a player (a) Play the ball, (b) Interfere with play, or (c) Gain advantage from a rebound? In this case your assistant is wrong: the offside player did not unsight the keeper before he was beaten, which would have counted as interfering, and he did not play the ball. So award the goal, but also have a word with your colleague, who should have delayed his flag.

22 This is an unsporting tactic from a manager who shouldn't be allowed in charge any of age group. Take control of the situation and inform the defending team's captain and manager that you have no intention of abandoning the game on false pretences and that there will be no replay. Their only chance to get anything from the final now is to get up and play for an equaliser. Tell the manager to leave the field of play and resume the match. Report everything that happened to the authorities.

23 When referees are registered, they have to give details of any club allegiance, so this should not happen. But if it does occur, exercise common sense and advise your colleague that you expect a completely impartial performance, and monitor him closely.

Page 24

24 The key point is that the substitution has technically been completed: one player has left the pitch and another has entered it. So the manager cannot choose a different player to go on instead. You need to ensure the injured player is treated and removed from the field of play, and then show the departing striker a red card for violent conduct. If the replacement had not put one foot on to the pitch a different sub could have been sent on in his place.

25 This is a clear error by your assistant. How you deal with it, depends on how quickly you realise your colleague has made a mistake. If you see the error while the move is in progress, signal and shout 'play on'. The striker should not have stopped until he heard your whistle. But if you have wrongly accepted the incorrect flag, you can only apologise and restart with a dropped ball.

26 First, ask if an alternative strip is available – or even a set of bibs – and if so, go ahead with the change. But if not, continue with the match anyway and report what was claimed after the game. You should also send the home manager to the stands. He cannot be allowed to charge onto the field to make demands.

Page 25

27 It's unconventional, but let him make the change. A substitution can be made at any time, provided the team has not used up its allocation. Allow him to make the change before the restart.

28 This has happened in the past but these days should not be possible as assistants are now told to operate on the right wing, and you should check with them before blowing for kick-off. But if this situation did arise, ask both assistants why they think the goal should or should not stand, and go with whichever opinion you judge to be correct. Restart with the assistants in their correct positions.

29 You've made a bad mistake here: you should not be basing any decisions on guesswork. It is too late, though, to withdraw the yellow card you've shown – if you did that, you would be effectively agreeing that there had been an act of violent conduct, which you also didn't see. So stand by the decision and then explain everything in your post-match report. You also cannot use the excuse of him removing his shirt for the second yellow – that is only an offence when celebrating a goal.

Page 26

30 This question shows how ready you need to be to think on your feet. The keeper has effectively handled the ball from a back pass without another player touching or playing the ball first. You should award an indirect free kick to be taken from where the keeper picked up the ball. But there is no need to show a yellow or red card for denying a goal-scoring opportunity, because keepers are allowed to handle the ball inside their penalty area.

31 These players may have been well meaning but it's not a laughing matter: both are guilty of unsporting behaviour. Disallow the goal, award both yellow cards, and restart the game with a dropped ball at the point where they removed their shirts.

32 This request is unacceptable. The coach must remain in the technical area during the shoot-out, so instruct him to return there before allowing any kicks to be taken.

Page 27

33 This situation provides a good test of your offside knowledge. The player who was struck in the face was in an offside position, but as he was behind the keeper he was not interfering with an opponent. However, as soon as he plays or touches the ball he becomes an active part of the game. Therefore when the ball hits him, blow and signal for offside. The goal is disallowed.

34 It's not illegal to be drunk on the field of play, but it is potentially unsafe and your priority as referee has to be safety. Start the second half, but if you notice that any players are behaving dangerously, you have the option to impose the usual individual sanctions and/or to abandon the game. You do not, however, have the power to order specific players to be substituted.

Page 28 Christian Eriksen

35 You don't have the power to interfere with team selection – that is the manager's domain and you and his players have to respect that. Clearly it's a volatile situation so you should explain all this calmly and try to keep a lid on their tempers. Resume the game with one team down to ten men as specified by their manager. Include everything in your post-match report.

36 This is a deliberate piece of cheating using violent conduct to gain an advantage. But this player knows the laws of the game well – you have no option but to send him off and allow a teammate to take his kick. If there is any justice, the striker will miss the kick, and his side will then have to put an outfield player in goal for the rest of the shootout.

37 The only factor you should consider here is the force of the shove. If it was violent, you have to intervene and send off the offending player, disallow the goal, and restart with an indirect free kick from where the contact took place. If you judge that the shove was a more minor contact, allow the goal, and keep a close eye on the two players to make sure there's no retaliation.

Page 29 Simon Mignolet

38 This devious trick does not create a valid goal. The keeper's fall was a direct result of the actions of the striker, who is clearly guilty of some pretty underhand unsporting behaviour. Disallow the goal, call the striker back, show him a yellow card, and restart with a free kick to the defending team that can be taken from anywhere inside the six-yard box.

39 An interesting problem, and another that shows the need to be ready to think on your feet and apply the laws as fairly as you can. The substitution, technically, has been completed – but a member of your team has made a genuine error, so I would show some common sense by allowing the substitution to be redone. However, you need to report the error to the authorities in your post-match report.

40 You can spare the player's blushes – this is not an own goal. The law on advantage is clear: you have to penalise the original offence if the anticipated advantage does not transpire in that immediate passage of play. So take play back to the original incident, and award a free kick at the position where the player was fouled.

Page 30 Brendan Rogers

41 You need to stop play. If the defender was going in for the tackle with the leg that was still protected by a shin pad, you could have allowed the passage of play to continue. But as it is, it's your primary job to protect players from causing danger to themselves or to others, so you have to intervene. Stop play, explain the situation, tell the defender to leave the pitch to re-insert the pad, and restart with a dropped ball.

42 The substitution wasn't complete when the offence took place. Swearing and abusive language aimed at the ref is a straight red card, so send him off, reducing his team to ten players. His manager will now have to decide which other player to bring off if he still wants to make a substitution.

43 There has been no offence, and play was still live, so some would say you should award the goal. But player safety is paramount so, even though you hadn't blown the whistle, you can consider that play stopped the moment the players collided. Call on the physios immediately, and have both players leave the pitch after treatment. Restart with a dropped ball.

Page 31 Michael Oliver

44 This is a valid goal. The referee is considered part of the field of play, so just as there'd be no reason to stop the game if a player leaned on a goalpost to stay upright, there's no reason to stop the game if he leans on you. There would be an offence only if the player was in any way violent or displaying dissent, or if he stopped you doing your job.

45 There are two main issues here. First, you cannot introduce new uses for the foam – it's only there for the management of free kicks. Secondly, you don't need to make dramatic gestures to deter dissent. You just need to impose firm and consistent sanctions. It's advisable always to consider cautioning any player guilty of dissent, and to always report any incident where three or more players surrounded you. The latter behaviour would be likely to lead to an FA charge. As for the manager, he may have a point, but any dissent from a manager should also be reported.

46 Your suspicions may be valid, but you cannot act on them. Spectator safety is paramount, and the decision is with the police and stadium officials, who would not want to risk disorder by allowing the game to kick-off with fans locked out. You should report the delay to all stakeholders, including the league, and, if the delay is longer than an hour, the game is likely to be postponed.

Page 32

47 Whatever the defender was or was not looking at when he launched himself, he has committed a reckless challenge. It's at least a yellow card offence, and possibly a red, if you rule it was serious foul play. As for the advert, all you can do is advise the player you will include his comments in your post-match report.

48 First, tell your fourth official that he should have shared this information with you straight away rather than five minutes later. Secondly, advise the player's manager that you intend to report what happened to the authorities so that they can investigate exactly what was administered, although there is nothing in the rules to stop players drinking coffee during stoppages, if they really think it'll help.

49 This is a serious concern and a growing problem in the game, but you don't have the authority to refuse permission for the player to continue. However, you must advise him and his manager that you will be reporting him after the game. The manager would be sensible to substitute him at that point.

Page 33

50 It's an own goal. In a situation like this, you should play advantage. If you were to award a free kick for handling, you'd be doing the defending team a favour they don't deserve.

51 There's no problem here. Although some referees penalise players in this situation, they're wrong to do so. Players are allowed to stand anywhere on the field, but they cannot move with the keeper, thereby preventing him from releasing the ball. And even then, the offence is not an automatic yellow card. You should book a player who moves with the keeper in this way only if the unsporting behaviour is overt – for example, raising his foot as the keeper kicks the ball.

52 Don't hesitate. You are the ref and – unless your assistants or the fourth official advise you to rethink the decision - you have to act on what you saw. Never take advice from players, however well intentioned it appears to be. Award the penalty, dismiss the defender, and have a strong word with the captain. It's worth noting, however, that the term 'last man' is not in the laws of the game – it's a media invention, and can confuse the way these situations are judged. What you're looking for is simply the denial of an obvious scoring opportunity.

Page 34

53 It doesn't matter which ball went into the net – you have no option but to disallow the goal due to outside interference. Restart with a dropped ball, which – given that this collision took place inside the six-yard box – should be taken from a position on the six-yard line parallel to the goal line and nearest to the point of contact. You also need to make sure that the ground staff have the ball boy escorted away. Be sure to include all the details in your post-match report.

54 You cannot tolerate this conduct or you will appear weak. If the captain is one of the three, address your remarks to him. If not, call him over and ask him to join the group. Tell him the language and tone used was unacceptable and would have led to a red card had the culprit been clearly identifiable. Ask him to remind his team of the laws of the game. Restart play with the penalty.

Page 35

55 The key consideration in any handball decision is whether the action was deliberate. In this case, the player's arm was not in a natural position, but the fact that his eyes were closed suggests it wasn't deliberate. You cannot award a penalty here. Play on.

56 Quickly get a grip and blow your whistle. You need to signal promptly and clearly that it's not a goal and apologise to both captains. You are considered part of the field of play – like a goalpost – so had the ball hit you accidentally and gone into the net it would have been a valid goal. But because you played the ball, the game has to be stopped. Restart with a dropped ball. After the match you must report yourself to the authorities. You can expect an extended break.

57 There's no offence here, so play on. The defender entered the area after the kick was taken, so if he can outpace the ball and reach it before it crosses the line, he's done nothing wrong. Equally, if a striker had entered the area after the kick was taken and reached the ball first, he would have been entitled to toe-poke it into the net for a valid goal.

Page 36 Jon Moss

58 You always have the option of handing over to a colleague for fitness reasons, or if you suspect that some other issue has clouded your judgement. But this is most definitely not one of those situations. Tell the players that if they refuse to continue, you will abandon the game and report the club to the authorities. It's a simple warning – if their actions cause the game to be called off, they can expect severe sanctions.

59 The manager made a sensible decision here. If the player had actually crossed the line, you would have had to show a second yellow card for leaving the field of play without permission – and therefore a red. But, given that play was not live, it makes sense to allow him to be subbed, despite the extremely late notice.

60 The defender's foul took place before the offside offence. You always punish the first offence, so the striker cannot be declared offside. In these circumstances, you should react to the first offence by playing advantage, even though the striker was in an offside position when he took control of the ball. Once the passage of play has concluded, show the defender a yellow card for unsporting behaviour.

Page 37

61 It counts as a miss. In open play a ball rebounding off you into the net would be a goal, as you're considered part of the field of play. However, while the laws on penalties make clear that a goal is awarded if the shot touches the keeper before going in, they also say that 'the referee decides when a penalty kick has been completed'. In these circumstances, it's right to consider the kick completed once the keeper runs out and boots the slowly trickling ball. So, the fact that it then hit you and went in is irrelevant.

62 First, stopping play was correct. The laws say that if an infringement warrants a red card, you must stop play and immediately send off the player unless there is subsequent opportunity to score. But, having played advantage, you cannot now award a penalty just because the teammate has messed about and fluffed their chance. So, make sure the fouled striker receives medical help, send the keeper off for serious foul play, and award a goal kick. Restart the game once a replacement keeper is in position.

63 If it's a competitive game, you have to abandon the match. It might seem sensible to allow a teammate to steady the ball, but the laws prevent teammates being inside the area when a penalty is taken. There's also no provision in the laws for the taker to improvise a way to secure the ball in the spot (with sand, for instance). It's a tough position to be in, but you have to make the decision.

Page 38 Anthony Taylor

64 You are the timekeeper, and if you say time is up, time is up. The game ends with the first of those three traditional peeps, not the last. However, referees are always advised to try to avoid this sort of row by blowing for full time when the ball is in a neutral area. In this instance, hanging on for a second or two would have avoided a bitter end to the game.

65 The player might think he is being clever here, but he's wrong. Disallow the goal for offside (he's deemed to be in an offside position from the point on the goal line where he re-entered) and show him a yellow card for unsporting behaviour. Restart with an indirect free kick on the six-yard line parallel to the goal line at the point nearest to where he re-joined play.

66 It's your decision. If you are sure the ball entered the goal, you must award it. Making tough calls is what you are there for. Explain the situation calmly to any players who dispute your decision, and sanction any who take their protest too far.

Page 39

67 Award a penalty. The line marking the edge of the area forms part of the area. You should also show the defender a yellow card for unsporting behaviour. A red would be appropriate if you think he prevented an obvious goal-scoring opportunity.

68 Your priority is safety. You have to be sure that the glasses do not present a risk of injury to the player or to others. The International FA Board (IFAB) has advised officials to show tolerance towards the use of modern sports spectacles, which are much safer for the wearer and for other players. But if they are a standard pair of glasses, you may have to intervene and ask the player to remove them.

69 Stop the game. Either show a yellow card or a red, depending on the severity of the challenge. For a foul to occur, the offence has to be committed on the field of play, but you must still deal with incidents that take place off it. The laws of the game make it clear that you cannot award a penalty in these circumstances. Restart the game with a dropped ball where the ball was when you blew the whistle (or on the six-yard line if it was inside the six-yard box).

Page 40 Kevin De Bruyne

70 Stop play immediately and send off both defenders for violent conduct. The striker has been badly let down by his colleagues here, their foolish behaviour has denied him the chance to score and reduced their team to nine men. What's more, they have also handed the opposition a great chance, as you have to restart play with an indirect free kick from where the defenders were fighting – inside their own penalty area.

71 Stop play and show the defender a yellow card. It's not a red card for denying an obvious goal-scoring opportunity because defenders are allowed to make clean tackles – his only offence here is coming on to the field without permission. Restart with an indirect free kick to the attacking team from where he entered play.

72 Without hesitation, show the defender a red card for his disgusting behaviour, and point to the penalty spot. This is the same situation as with a sliding challenge, which begins outside the penalty area but makes contact with an opponent inside the area. The offence takes place at the point of contact.

Page 41

73 The keeper cannot touch the ball after it has been deliberately kicked to him by a teammate, but that's not the case here, so you do not need to take any action. But keep an eye on them in case they try it again. If it turns out to be a deliberate ruse to get around the back pass law, you need to warn the players. Tell the keeper he will be penalised if it happens again.

74 As the referee, you must base your decisions on what you have seen. First, call on medical help. Secondly, deal with the defender's actions. If you did not notice the blood before the handball, award a penalty and send off the defender for denying an obvious goal-scoring opportunity. If you spotted the blood first, you have the option to rule that the game stopped at that instant on safety grounds, and to restart with a dropped ball. A big decision.

75 No goal. Part of your management of a penalty kick is to identify the taker. Once that has happened, no other player can take the kick. Award a retake, while explaining to both attacking players why the goal cannot stand.

Page 42

76 Arrange medical help for the injured sub, then deal with what happened. You didn't see the incident and you're not allowed to use television evidence during a match, but you can ensure that the video evidence is retained. Advise both clubs that you will be reporting the incident to the authorities. Note that the injured sub cannot be replaced on the bench by another squad member as the game is under way.

77 Get medical attention for the defender, and then show him a red card for denying an obvious goal-scoring opportunity. Although the striker caused the injury, it was accidental – the defender's action was deliberate. Restart with a direct free kick to the attacking side or, if the incident took place inside the area, award a penalty.

78 This is poor refereeing – you should have stopped play and ordered a retake when the wall crossed the line. As it is, you've now no choice but to rule the attacker offside. When he received the ball in that position, he was gaining an advantage, and so must be penalised. It's tough on him, and reflects badly on you, but you have to restart with an indirect free-kick to the defenders.

Page 43 Petr Cech

79 You can't award the goal. The player has knocked it in from an offside position, so his side have failed to take the advantage you correctly played. Instead, take the game back to the position of the goalkeeper's offence, and show him a yellow card for his unsporting behaviour. Restart with a direct free kick to the attacking team.

80 It's clear that the player wants to skip his kick so that his team's penalty specialist take it for him. That can't happen. Speak to his captain and explain clearly that if the player refuses to participate, you will abandon the game. And tell him that, if the game is called off for this reason, the authorities will award the match to the opposition.

81 Tell this attacker he'll be booked if he walks off the field of play without permission. You should also explain to him that there is nothing in the laws of the game that means a tackle is only rash and dangerous if physical contact is made. Tripping or attempting to trip an opponent is an offence, so if this defender has launched himself into a dangerous challenge, he has earned a red card for reckless play with excessive force even if there was no contact.

Page 44 Riyad Mahrez

82 Stop the throw being taken. The offence here is the manager entering the field of play. Have a word with the manager, who should know better. Restart with a dropped ball from the position where he entered the pitch.

83 First, the easy bit: send them both off. Next, you need to deal with the starting line-ups. Because the game had not begun when you showed the red cards, both managers can now convert a named substitute from their original team sheets into a starting player. It means they will now each have one fewer sub to choose from during the game, but they can still make three changes. Once everyone is clear and the two teams have new captains, resume the coin toss as normal.

84 It's always a priority to avoid penalising a team who have done nothing wrong, but there are times when you have no choice. This is one of those times. You cannot award the goal here because play was 'dead' the moment the boy touched the ball. Make sure the boy is removed from pitch side, and restart with a dropped ball. This should be taken from where the boy made contact with the ball or, if he was inside the six-yard box, at a point on the goal area line parallel to the goal line nearest to where he touched the ball. Keep everyone calm and explain the rules. Include full details in your post-match report.

Page 45 Kasper Schmeichel

85 If a player removes his shirt to celebrate a goal he must be cautioned – no exceptions. As he has disappeared down the tunnel already, you'll have to advise him in the dressing room that he has earned a second yellow. Request a stadium announcement to tell the crowd what has happened, and that his team will play the second half with ten men. You may also need to report him for leaving the field without permission (another yellow card offence) if he crossed the line before you blew for half time.

86 The player was out of control, so you have to show him a second yellow card, followed by a red. Players should understand that they have a duty of care towards their opponents. As for the striker, have a strong word with him. You don't need his advice on how to referee the game, and by failing to take evasive action, he has endangered himself for no good reason. The defender would have been cautioned for his reckless challenge whether or not contact was made.

87 Tell the keeper to calm down and then check with your assistant in case he saw anything you missed. Assuming he didn't, the goal stands. You can only work on the confirmed information available to you and all you know for sure is that the goal-line technology registered that the ball had crossed the line. You can't base your decisions on mysterious patterns on the ball.

Page 46 Gary Neville

88 Award the goal. There's no need to consult your assistant first – the goal-line technology in the Premier League is foolproof. It's most likely that the ball will have hit one post and, in ricocheting to hit the other, looped over the line. It's clearly possible for you to miss a spin like that. Your wrist buzzer will only have triggered if the whole of the ball had crossed the line. This is a clear decision that is not in your hands.

89 IFAB rules prohibit players displaying 'political, religious or personal slogans', and players are punished for celebrations that deliberately provoke fans. However, gestures like this are seen all the time, all over the world, and you have to show some common sense. Award the goal, but be sure to include details of the celebration and the consequent protest in your post-match report.

90 Yes, you certainly do need to interfere. Show the penalty taker a yellow card for delaying the restart of the game with this obvious show of unsporting behaviour.

Page 47

91 The manager is wrong. The technical area isn't his own personal empire. According to the laws of the game, it's simply a designated zone from where he can convey tactical instructions while 'behaving in a responsible manner'. Ask him to stand aside to allow the player space to take the kick. If he fails to comply, send him to the stands for delaying the restart.

92 The simplest way to approach this is to say that one of these two throws was clearly taken from the wrong position. Stop play and restart with a throw to the opposition from the correct spot, have a quiet word with the over-eager ball boys.

93 Caution the teammate for dissent and award an indirect free kick to the defending side. It was your decision to play advantage, and it should not be undermined by the players. This player has turned an attacking position into a defending position, and earned himself a yellow card. Hopefully he will learn the lesson.

Page 48 Zlatan Ibrahimovic

94 Show two yellows, then a red. But it's poor game management. It's always a risk to play advantage after a bookable offence. It's best to do it only when the next kick of the ball would either go into the net or would set up a clear goal-scoring opportunity. But whenever you play advantage in these circumstances, you should always make every effort to shout to the player concerned that he has committed a yellow card offence as play continues, to avoid this sort of dispute.

95 Snug-fitting tops are increasingly common and there's no reason to intervene here. The law on equipment says that players cannot wear anything that is dangerous, and stipulates the basic kit as a jersey or shirt with sleeves, plus shorts, socks, shin guards and footwear. This kit does not contravene any obvious section of the law, so you should let them wear it.

96 The player's ponytail has to be considered part of his person and there's nothing in the rules about the maximum permitted length of hair. The indirect free kick has touched a player on its way into the net, and no outside agent has been involved. It's a goal.

Page 49

97 This is a difficult call and there is no firm rule to assist you, but the following is a valid approach. If, after treatment, the player and physio both say he is fine to carry on playing, then it would be fair to assume it wasn't a serious medical incident, and that he was sufficiently in control of himself for you to conclude that he deliberately denied an obvious goal. In this situation, show him a red card and award a penalty. But if the medical staff say that the player cannot carry on, you should accept that it wasn't a deliberate handball, and award a corner.

98 This is a decision that requires sensitive judgement. The scoreline clearly points to the risk of some gamesmanship here. If you genuinely believe the team are not trying to con you, and that emotions are too raw, then you do have the option to abandon the game. If, however, you have doubts, you should ask the two teams to play out the remainder of the game. If the home side refuse, then you will have to abandon, including full details in your report so that the authorities can investigate.

99 If a foul starts outside the area and continues into it, you have the option to play advantage from the initial foul and penalise the 'continued offence' inside the area. That is what you should do here: award the penalty.

Page 50

100 It's irrelevant to whom they are directing foul abuse – it's not acceptable. Swearing can be a difficult issue but swearing as part of directed personal abuse is not something you can or should tolerate. If possible, identify the ringleader and send him off. If there are two players who are equally guilty of the worst abuse, show both of them red cards.

101 There are times as a referee when showing some common sense and a relaxed attitude makes sense in terms of game-management – and this is one of those times. The coin toss was carried out correctly, albeit in a roundabout way, so take no action and start the game – after you've asked for your coin back.

102 You need more information before you react. Stop play if the ball isn't already dead and then seek the views of both of your assistants. If they were certain this body charge was a deliberate act, then quite clearly you need to show the player a red card for violent conduct. If, however, they cannot be sure, let it go, and include an account of the incident in your report. The authorities may choose to review video evidence.

Page 51 Troy Deeney

103 Your key role as a referee is to make correct, clear decisions, and to do that you need accurate information from your assistants. So, if this assistant needs to come on to the field in order to keep up with play then he should do so, especially when the ball is not close. Explain this to the defenders, and ask them to get on with the game. Another option, if the surface is really bad, is to ask your two assistants to run the left wings instead.

104 No markings other than those specified in the laws of the game are permitted. Delay the restart until the keeper's line is removed, and the original lines are uncovered. It's not unknown for ground staff to use dye to make lines more visible in the winter. But if it proves impossible to make the pitch markings visible and the surface playable, then abandonment may be the right call.

105 Whatever his motives – and you're far too busy to be mind reading – the rules are clear: you must issue him with a yellow card. You can't pick and choose which laws to enforce, but you can include full details of what happened in your post-match report.

Page 52

106 You can't ignore this. You've witnessed the manager striking another person off the field of play. When he returns to his technical area, dismiss him to the stands for misconduct. This may also be a matter for the police and security staff. If you had to stop the game to take action, restart with a dropped ball. Include full details in your post-match report.

107 It's a corner. The goalkeeper rightly tried to avoid handling the ball from the deliberate back pass – he only intervened with his hand in a second phase of play, after the ball had rebounded off the post. This is a good example of how alert and quick thinking you have to be.

108 You have split seconds to sort this one out in your mind. In my view, the key factors are these (a) The striker was onside when the ball was played, (b) The defender was not fouled when he fell to the ground and (c) The defender was not seriously impeded when the striker tried to pick him up – he was already lying down. Therefore, I see no reason to penalise the attacking side, so award the goal. You should, though, warn both players against using exaggerated gestures to try and influence decisions – tell them that you are the ref.

Page 53 Zinedine Zidane

109 First things first, the captain cannot 'insist' you do anything, so make this clear to him. Next, give him a lesson in the laws. The guidance on players leaving the pitch after treatment includes some commonsense written exceptions. One is that keepers are exempt. Another states that if a keeper and an attacker collide and both need attention, both are exempt, to avoid unfairly disadvantaging the attacking side. In the same way, if a keeper and one of his teammates collide and both need treatment, both stay on, to avoid unfairly disadvantaging the defending side. So, in this case, all three players stay on as play restarts.

110 It's a mess, but you can't start undoing the damage now. Ask the player for his name. If it matches the name of the player you booked in the first half, send him off. If he gives you a different name, show him a yellow and continue as normal. Report everything to the authorities after the game. Either way, he and his club will face sanctions. Sadly, so may you, for not spotting the problem sooner.

111 The manager has no right to intervene. As the referee, you have a duty of care, and if the player tells you he needs treatment then you must make sure he gets it. Once the player has been treated, ask him to leave the field in the normal way. Report the manager after the game.

Page 54 Dele Alli

112 If you saw the incident, and it was deliberate, this physio has to be removed from the pitch and the technical area. If you didn't see it, you cannot assume deliberate wrongdoing. Either way, calm everyone down and make it clear that the incident will be in your report, and that the authorities will use video evidence to establish the facts. As for what happens next, the rules allow you to delay the restart while a goalkeeper is being treated, so you can allow time for him to recover before resuming play.

113 It's a goal. This player's hair, whether real or artificial, counts as part of his person. But, now that you are aware that the bun is poorly attached, before restarting play, you need to have a word with the player. Tell him that if he wants to continue, he has to play without it, as it could pose a safety risk.

114 You should have intervened faster to stop him damaging the spot so badly. As it is, you have two options: either have ground staff perform a quick fix, or move the remainder of the shoot-out to the other end of the pitch. As for the defender, his actions were obviously unsporting, so show him a second yellow card, followed by a red. His side will be reduced to ten men.

Page 55 Eddie Howe

115 This is a really unfortunate situation, but you have to try to calm everyone down and explain the position. The match officials are considered part of the field of play – in the same way as the goalposts or corner flag posts. So, if the ball makes contact with you, even involving an instinctive action such as this, the game continues. You have to award the goal.

116 You cannot intervene. The game's authorities have imposed a stadium ban, and they are the ones who must judge what further action to take. Simply advise the club's secretary that you have seen what is happening and will be including it in your report. Then start the game as normal.

117 You must take action when racist abuse is unequivocal. Options include requesting stadium announcements, taking the teams off, and potentially abandoning the game. But you need to be sure of the facts. In this case, explain your concerns to both captains, and tell them that, in any case, after the match you will be reporting what has occurred so that the authorities can conduct a proper investigation. What is more, UEFA competitions always have a match delegate present who monitors crowd behaviour.

Page 56 Fraser Foster

118 You need to stop play, but not because the shirt is the wrong way around. He went off under Law 4, which concerns players' equipment, so he cannot return until the ball is out of play, and you have checked the condition of the new shirt. Stop the game, show him a yellow card for coming back on without your permission, and then have him adjust his shirt so that the number is visible. Restart with an indirect free kick to the opposition, taken from the point where the ball was when you stopped play.

119 It's all about safety here. You have to determine whether these leather ridges could represent more of a danger to this player and his opponents than conventional studs. Judging from their appearance, there seems to be no additional safety risk here, so allow the player to go ahead and wear them. It would have been better if the team had made you aware of them before the start of the game.

120 It's a normal throw to the opposition. The ball entered the field of play in a legal way, and the last player who touched it was the throw-taker. It's a similar situation to that of a long-throw specialist who somehow manages to throw the ball out over the opposite touchline. There's no offence to punish.

Page 57

121 Stop the game. The ball has to be in the quadrant or touching its line. You should have the ground staff sweep away the water until the ball can be positioned to your satisfaction for a legal corner. If that doesn't work, suspend play to allow time for staff to work on the corner area with forks and sand. If that is ineffective, you'll have to abandon the game.

122 Swallow your pride, admit your mistake and withdraw the red card. Apologise to the player, but also tell him that you will not tolerate any further confrontational behaviour. To avoid this sort of error, referees are always instructed to take names when issuing cautions.

123 Call the players over and, if the seriousness of the physical confrontation warrants it, issue a caution to each of them. Remind them that it's your responsibility to take the match ball off the field of play at the end of the game, after which you will hand it over to home officials. What the home club does with it after that is down to them.

Page 58 Rafael Benitez

124 Goal. It's not what most people would call sporting behaviour, but it doesn't qualify as unsporting behaviour in the strict terms of the laws of the game. The goalkeeper must be alert at all times and, as every youngster knows, play to the whistle.

125 You have to base your decisions on what you and your colleagues see or hear in real time. As things stand, referees cannot use video footage to judge an incident, so all you can do is reassure the manager that the authorities will investigate and take action if the abuse is proven. Keep a close eye on the players involved in the second half. This is the type of scenario that the use of VAR would detect.

126 No goal. You should have stopped play the moment the ball reached the player you planned to dismiss – he shouldn't be on the pitch and you cannot allow him to benefit from the advantage you awarded the opposition. Call him over and show him a second yellow, then a red. Restart with an indirect free kick, taken from the location of the ball when it reached him. This is the point at which you should have stopped play.

Page 59

127 There's not a lot you can do. The home side may think they're doing the noble thing, but their actions have skewed the competition and, if the authorities allow the result to stand, will result in another team being unfairly relegated. All you can do at the end is inform officials from both sides that you will be reporting the conduct of the players involved.

128 This is poor refereeing. You can only apologise for restarting play too soon, and award a retake. You could also caution the player who was subbed, if you feel he was deliberately trying to delay the restart by leaving the pitch unreasonably slowly.

129 You can't stop him if he really wants to do this, but you shouldn't condone it. Technically it is legal for the 11th player named on the team sheet to come on at a later stoppage in the game – in this case, the 11th minute – and his team will still have three subs to use. But this type of gimmick makes a mockery of the game. Tell the manager that if he starts with ten men you will report him.

Page 60

130 Time for some common sense. It's a head injury, but there's no need to stop play. The player landed off the pitch, he's already receiving medical attention, and – even after he rolled back on – neither he nor the physio is interfering with play. So, await the outcome of the attack, and then stop the game. Delay the restart until the injury has been fully dealt with. You also need to consider the defender's behaviour. Did he roll back on due to momentary confusion caused by his injury or was it a deliberate attempt to disrupt the opposition attack? You have to be very certain of the latter possibility before taking any action against him. However, if you are sure, show him a yellow card for entering the field of play without permission.

131 The rules are clear – only the players who were on the field of play at the end of the game can be involved in the shoot-out. So, before the kicks begin, equalise the numbers in the two teams. In this case, they'll have ten takers each. This is one of those situations where the club staff clearly don't know the laws properly.

132 You are the decision maker – so make your decision and stick by it. You need to have the self-belief to act on what you and your colleagues saw, and nothing else. If you don't think the keeper touched it, award a goal kick.

Page 61

133 Yes. When officials are appointed to games they're expected to be professional and impartial, whatever the circumstances. But keep an eye on him. If during the match, he indicates through act or word that he's unable to act neutrally, then ask him to step down, appoint a replacement, and report what happened. A professional is perfectly capable of being impartial in these sorts of situations.

134 This is a tight call. Has the original ball directly interfered with play? If you are 100 per cent certain it has, you cannot award the goal, but otherwise you should give it. Never penalise a team who have done nothing wrong unless it's absolutely unavoidable.

135 Treat the crowd abuse just as you'd treat racist chanting. You should request a stadium announcement to give a warning. If the abuse continues in the second half, you have the option at that point to suspend the game and, ultimately, to abandon it. As for the manager, check with your colleagues. If any official heard any of these alleged remarks, send the manager to the stands and report him. If not, tell him an allegation has been made which will be reported for investigation. Show your full support to the player concerned and reassure him you are dealing with the situation.

Page 62 Alexis Sanchez

136 Assuming the throw wasn't unduly hard or intended to cause injury, the attacker hasn't committed any offence here, so award the goal. As for the defender, he didn't actually delay the restart, so he avoids a booking this time. But warn him that if he does this again, he'll be cautioned. The laws require him to be at least two metres away from the point at which the ball is thrown, and you can remind him of that.

137 You and your assistants are considered part of the field of play, so any collision like this is considered a 'play on' situation, especially when it is accidental. As for the offside call, you can base your decisions only on what you and your colleagues have seen. You cannot disallow a goal based on a hunch, and your assistant was in no position to contribute. So award the goal and check that your assistant is not injured.

138 You cannot award the goal. You should always delay a decision in cases like this. Having blown the whistle, you now have to follow through and award the penalty. You then need to decide whether to send the keeper off. Technically, he did not deny a goal-scoring opportunity because the ball rolled into the net. Only your poor refereeing prevented a goal being scored at that point. But, having awarded the penalty, meaning the game stopped when the foul was committed, you should dismiss him. For the ref, it's a self-inflicted mess.

Page 63

139 You can't allow the captain to get away with this: caution him, or show him a red card if you feel his action involved excessive force. After checking on the wellbeing of the injured player and telling the away team's physio in no uncertain terms to calm down, have a word with their captain too. Make it clear that any time-wasting tactics will be dealt with firmly. As always, include full details in your post-match report.

140 If you let this go with just a warning, you'll be making the situation even worse for yourself. You have to show him a yellow card for dissent, because he's clearly undermining your authority. You need to have courage to make this type of difficult decision.

141 Make a decision and stick to it. It's important to be clear, confident and decisive. You can make a case for either decision. The attacking team would obviously favour a corner, but a throw would be the safest, least controversial option, and therefore preferable.

Page 64 Cristiano Ronaldo

142 It's a goal. There's obviously no offside here, and any appeals are pretty desperate. You should rule that the striker's action represented deliberate violent conduct only if he had fired the ball in a manner clearly intended to cause injury. As it is, there is no convincing reason to disallow the goal.

143 Calm things down and have a word with the away team's staff. The priority here is to get the game played, and there are various options. If there's time, it might be possible to source a spare set of shirts outside the ground. If not, the visitors could borrow a change strip from the home club, provided there are no issues with sponsors. Failing that, tell them to play with their own shirts turned inside out. Not ideal, but good enough. The fact that there are no names and numbers visible on the shirts should not stop the game from going ahead.

144 Your fourth official has exceeded his responsibilities here. He cannot sanction substitutions independently just because you are busy. Tell him firmly that he has made a difficult situation worse. Next, as play has not restarted, ask the substitute to leave the field of play. Then request a stadium announcement to make it clear to the crowd that the injured player was dismissed. The fact that you did not actually brandish a red card before the player left the pitch is irrelevant.

Page 65

145 You need to judge the mood. If the captain was obviously joking and the tone is light, laugh it off, but tell him enough is enough and start the game. If he reacts badly or persists with the 'joke', then show him a yellow card, but avoid giving a caution if you can – it could lead to an uneasy 90 minutes.

146 Goal. A keeper can score goals and is allowed to use his hands inside his own area, so there's no offence here. But you also need to consider whether to abandon the game if the weather is having such an impact on play. What's more, high winds could potentially pose a safety risk – another reason why you may be forced to call off the game.

147 They have a point, it does seem unfair, but once a minimum of six added minutes has been shown, you have to play them. Patiently explain the rules to the home players, and tell them you have done everything in your power to cancel out the effects of the time wasting. Now it's up to them to protect their lead.

Page 66

148 There's not much you can do about the fans, but you can be proactive and address the behaviour of the players. Delay the kick and call over the attacking side's captain. Let him know that if his players continue, you will start cautioning them for what is clearly unsporting behaviour.

149 It's a goal. One of the first lessons drilled into every youngster by youth coaches is to 'play to the whistle'. The keeper's rather arrogant failure to do this has cost his side a goal. Players are allowed to leave the field without permission during open play if they're doing so in order to beat an opponent.

150 Ignore the defenders' complaints. It's up to them to defend the kick and there's nothing in the laws to stop opponents standing near a defensive wall providing they don't attempt to break it physically. Award the goal – the ball deflected off a defender. Ignore the defenders' complaints – they are expected to do their job and defend.

Page 67

151 This sustained attempt to undermine you is dissent. Make it clear that if he continues you will caution him. You need to be tough. While captains are allowed to approach referees, you must treat them as you would any other player. Do not allow your authority to be questioned.

152 You have no choice but to send off the away captain for serious foul play and abandon the game. A game must not continue if one side has fewer than seven players. But action will be taken against the player and his team after the match. The regulations allow the authorities to declare a winner if over 60 minutes have been played.

153 There is no goal. The attacking player deliberately moved the post to gain an unfair advantage. Disallow the goal, show the striker a yellow card, and restart with an indirect free kick to the defending team from the corner quadrant.

Page 68 Heurelho Gomes

154 In this situation, you must show the penalty-taker a yellow card for unsporting behaviour and record a missed penalty kick. This kind of play risks undermining the validity of a penalty shoot-out.

155 As a goal was scored, the defender can't be said to have denied an obvious goal-scoring opportunity. You must award the goal and then show him a yellow card for deliberate handball. The defender cleverly saved himself from a sending off at no real expense to his side who are comfortably ahead.

156 Your decision needs to be based on a judgement as to whether the defender denied an obvious goal-scoring opportunity (DOGSO). You must consider if the striker would have been able to control the ball when he collected it, whether he was moving towards goal, and given that he was 40 yards from goal, would any other defender have been able to dispossess him before he got the chance to shoot? If you were to decide based on those factors that it was not a DOGSO, you would give a direct free kick and caution the defender for unsporting behaviour. But if you think there was a genuine chance that the striker could have scored, as is probable in this case, you must show the defender a red card and restart with a direct free kick.

Page 69

157 Try to escort him off, but if that fails, show the defender a second yellow card and then a red. You must also stop the substitute coming on. Restart play in the normal way. You will have stopped your watch so no playing time has been lost.

158 Yes, it is a goal. This is a quick free kick – not a more formal 'ceremonial' kick, which involves pacing out ten yards for the wall. A quick free kick is a chance for an attacking team to get on with play, if they spot an opportunity. Inevitably this means defending players will sometimes be fewer than ten yards away when the kick is taken. The attacking side have asked to take the kick quickly despite knowing a defender is nearby, and you have sanctioned it. The taker has turned the situation to his advantage. The taker has done nothing wrong, so it would be bizarre to penalise him by disallowing the goal. The only situation where you would intervene is if the taker had blasted the ball at the defender using excessive force, thereby risking injury.

159 Dismiss these protests. The attacking team are just being opportunistic. For a handball offence to be committed, it has to be deliberate, and this clearly isn't.

Page 70 Ian Holloway

160 Yes. If the dimensions of the pitch are correct, the playing surface is safe, and the markings are clear, there's no problem with different coloured markings. Officials always want to get matches played if it's safe to do so.

161 It's an own goal by the keeper. A goal can only be scored from an indirect free kick if a player, other than the taker, has touched the ball. In this case, the keeper, in his fury, has done so. You should also show him a yellow card for dissent.

Page 71 Lionel Messi

162 What are you doing checking Twitter at half time! You should be focused on preparing for the second half. But now that you've had a look and seen the message, you simply need to rise above it – you cannot deal with this during the match, but you can include it in your post-match report to the authorities.

163 Play advantage in the usual way, and once the passage of play ends, stop the game and issue the player with a second yellow card and a red. Then abandon the game and report the full facts to the authorities.

164 Allow the forward to continue. He hasn't committed an infringement, and so should not be penalised. The defender clearly should have played on. Rather than trying to get you to break up the attack for them, he should have handed the scissors to you the next time the ball went out of play. If anything, he has made the situation more dangerous by picking the scissors up and waving them around.

Page 72

165 Send the substitute off. The law was amended in 2006 to cover a red card for a sub or substituted player who denies a goal. His team will now have one fewer subs to choose from, but will continue to play with 11 players. You could award a penalty only if the handling offence was committed by an active outfield player. As the offence was by a sub, restart with an indirect free kick from the six-yard line parallel to the goal line at a point nearest to where the offence occurred.

166 Both players have committed an offence. Show the striker a yellow card for delaying the restart and show the keeper a red card. Once the defending team have replacement keeper in place, restart with an indirect free kick for the original offside decision.

167 Play on. The goalkeeper has not committed an offence, removing a shirt is only a yellow card offence when done specifically in celebration of a goal, or if you deem it could have incited opposition fans. This keeper is celebrating in front of his own fans. It may seem an anomaly, but you need to stick to the letter of the law.

Page 73 Ole Gunnar Solskjaer

168 Players should be focused enough not to be put off by distractions like this – stadiums are not quiet places. But this still counts as outside interference. Guidelines state that there should be no public announcements (other than in an emergency) or music played during a game. And here there is also a pretty clear suspicion it was a deliberate attempt to distract. Have a word with the stadium manager, then allow the penalty to be retaken. Include the incident in your post-match report.

169 Award a penalty. The defender has committed an offence by holding his opponent. And you should not be worrying about what might have happened next had that offence not taken place. This isn't a guessing game.

170 As always, base your decision on what you have observed, not on what players are claiming. If you have not heard any racist chanting, award a direct free kick outside the area and advise the keeper that you will monitor the situation. If you have heard the chants, stop play and either restart with a dropped ball or consider taking the teams off, depending on the severity of the abuse. Whatever action you take, you should also liaise with the stadium manager so that more stewards can be placed in the relevant area. Report what happened to the authorities after the game.

Page 74

171 This is a close call. For purposes of judging handballs, the 'hand' is deemed to extend up the arm to the point at the shoulder where the shirt sleeve is stitched on. So, in this case. I would rule that the player has not deliberately used his arm to stop the shot. The fact that the ball then ricocheted down on to the lower arm is irrelevant. When the ball hits the body and then the hand, it is not a deliberate handball. So, there is no penalty – play on.

172 Yes, this is permissable. The defender was injured as a result of a clash with a goalkeeper. The law on players having to leave the field of play to receive treatment excludes cases when a goalkeeper and player have collided and need attention.

173 The keeper is right. Spitting is unacceptable. It's a red card offence if it's aimed at an opponent or official. In this case, caution the spitter for unsporting behaviour, have the ball cleaned or replaced, then proceed with the penalty.

Page 75

174 A tough call. Instead of removing his shirt – an automatic yellow card offence – he's put another one on. But if he has unnecessarily delayed the restart, he should still be shown a second yellow. I would try to avoid that, but if he really does cause a hold-up, you have little option. If you do give him the benefit of the doubt, make sure he removes the new shirt before play resumes.

175 Yes. Unless you are playing advantage, stop play, and caution the player for unsporting behaviour. Taking a phone onto the field of play could present a danger. Once you've shown him a yellow card, order him from the field, restart with an indirect free-kick. Allow the player to return, without the phone, when the ball is next out of play.

176 If the goal-line technology has not registered a goal and you and your assistant are not sure that the whole of the ball has crossed the line then you cannot award a goal. Stop play and treat the bottle as an outside agent by awarding a dropped ball on the goal area line parallel to the goal line. Make sure the keeper places the bottle in the back of the net before resuming play.

Page 76 Garry Monk

177 The language and the gesture may not be overtly abusive, but any goading relating to issues of race or sexuality is clearly offensive, and therefore must not be tolerated. Referees are now empowered to dismiss players for language or gestures that are offensive, and this certainly applies here. Do not hesitate to show a red card to the player making the comments.

178 Goal. The keeper is on the field to keep goal, not to police the game. Play was live, so the goal stands. Maybe you should have been faster to stop play when the players clashed, and maybe the striker who scored has been less than sporting here – but, as always, everyone needs to remember to play to the whistle.

179 You and your officials have badly messed up here. You should have checked that your assistants were correctly positioned before signalling for kick-off. But as it is, the offside decision is now yours alone to make. You cannot disallow a goal simply on a suspicion, so you have to award it. Once your assistants are in the correct positions, restart in the normal way, and include the details in your report.

Page 77

180 An interesting one. Before the game starts teams must fill out a form detailing who will be in the technical area, but there is no requirement that those named must actually stay in the technical area at all times. So you have no grounds to prevent this approach. Your assistants will have checked the subs' equipment before kick-off, and the fourth official will deal with the substitution process during the game. But make sure that the equipment is checked again before players come on.

181 The game has not restarted, so you can change your mind. Controversial incidents are not supposed to be shown on big screens, but it is important your decisions are correct. So based on what you saw, disallow the goal and explain what has happened to the players. The club can expect a sanction for breaking the rules on replays.

182 Call the keeper and his captain over to you, away from the incident, and tell them that as you did not hear anything, you will not be taking immediate action, but you will be reporting what has been alleged to the authorities. You should also ask the ground controller to place extra security behind the goal.

Page 78 Arsene Wenger & Steve Bruce

183 You need to be ready for anything. In theory, this should not happen. According to competition rules, these details should be set out well in advance. For UEFA games, a meeting takes place at 10.30 am on the day to check team colours, logo sizes, ball boy colours, warm up bib colours, and other details. However, there is nothing in the rules to stop teams changing to an alternative strip at half time, unless it would mean a colour clash. You can therefore allow the swap to take place.

184 It's all in the timing. If you were whistling as the defender caught the ball, that's fine. You can arrange treatment and restart with a dropped ball. But if you hadn't blown the whistle in time, you need to take action. Players should not take the law into their own hands, whatever the motive. In this case you have to award a penalty kick, signal for the medics to come on, and if the ball was going in, show the defender a red card.

185 Play the game. The colour of line markings is not stipulated in the laws – they just need to be distinct. Clubs often use green sand to cover any confusing lines.

Page 79 Hugo Lloris

186 There's no need to stop the game just because the colliding players are from the same team. But when the ball is next out of play, the procedure for dealing with the injuries is different from that used when the players are from opposing teams. Call the physio(s) on, then restart in the usual way with both players still on the pitch. The players do not need to go off before the restart. The rules are clear that this requirement is void when players from the same team have collided and need immediate attention.

187 There's nothing in the rules about boot colour, but socks have to comply with the team colours, and players can't mix and match from his side's home and away strips. If the club's strip features different coloured socks let him continue. If not, ask him to leave the pitch and replace the one that doesn't comply with the strip.

188 This is a very serious situation. As only 15 minutes have been played, speak to the offending team's manager and captain and tell them that you are restarting the second half with only the three valid changes and with the score reset to what it was at half time. The original twin can stay on. It's obviously a huge step to take, but you have that power. Your other option is to have the substitute twin removed, and tell them to complete the game with ten men. Either way, report everything to the authorities after the game.

Page 80 Joachim Low

189 The defender is considered to be on the goal line, so the attacker is onside and play continues. When the phase of play is complete, show the defender a yellow card for unsporting behaviour (leaving the field of play without permission).

190 The defender's quick thinking has saved him. He has not denied a goal, so there is no red card offence. Award the goal, and then show the defender a yellow card for his deliberate handball.

191 It goes without saying that this is something that should have been sorted out before kick-off. Teams should definitely not play with the same coloured sleeves due to the problems that can arise when you're trying to judge handballs. Because there is a long time before half time, have a word with the away side's bench, ask them to prepare an alternative strip urgently, and then suspend play at the first opportunity to allow for a change. If there's a problem with providing the alternative strip speedily, carry on until half time, and then make the change.

Page 81 Mauricio Pochettino

192 Apart from ordering the watering to stop if you notice in time, this is one of those situations you really cannot address during the game. So play the second half, advising both teams that the matter will be reported to the authorities afterwards. UEFA always take a very active approach to this issue, establishing pitch-watering plans on the morning of matches to try and avoid this sort of problem.

193 The winger clearly means well, but he has forgotten the first piece of advice given to every young player: play to the whistle. It is up to you, as referee, to stop the game if there's a serious injury. However, you should not ignore your suspicion about the defender's behaviour. Speak to his manager and tell him you will be reporting the apparently feigned collapse.

194 A substitution is the club's decision – it's really up to them to resolve it. Calm everyone down and ask the players and their manager come to an agreement quickly. If the dispute continues, inform the manager and the captain that, if they cannot resolve the situation promptly, you will abandon the game and report them. That should focus minds.

Page 82

195 The player is being petulant, but he hasn't committed an offence. A penalty is considered taken when the ball is kicked and moves forwards. But the timekeeping is entirely up to you. So go ahead and blow for full time if stoppage time is indeed up. But if not, tell the players to play on. It means the taker has potentially made his side vulnerable to a counterattack.

196 Your first priority is safety – get the player away from the crowd and monitor the situation in the stands to make sure stewards are restoring order. Once you are both away from the flashpoint area, show the player a yellow card for inciting the crowd. It's unacceptable – and dangerous.

197 This is a clear abuse of what is known as the multi ball system. While you cannot have the system withdrawn mid match, you should talk to the ball boys and the home manager and tell them that if the abuse continues, the club will be reported. You should also speak to both captains and tell them you will add an appropriate amount of time to cover the delays so far. And don't forget to have a firm word with the player who was shouting. He shouldn't behave like this towards the youngsters, who are clearly acting on instruction.

Page 83 Eden Hazard

198 If it's a valid complaint, it's an issue you should have spotted before the game: team colours are agreed and inspected in advance. But to avoid the risk of controversy and complaints, stop play and request the keeper change his shirt to a neutral colour.

199 It's not for managers or players to pick and choose which laws of the game suit them best. Tell him you will be refereeing as you see fit, and, as advantage is part of the law, you'll be applying it where appropriate. You should also tell him that you'll be reporting his approach to the authorities for them to determine if they wish to take any action. While he's not trying to fix the game, this manager is trying to influence how it is officiated, and there has to be a zero-tolerance approach to such interventions.

200 The fact that you have signalled for full time does not invalidate the events in the seconds leading up to the final whistle. The technology has told you that the ball crossed the line before you blew, so you have to award the goal, provided there were no offences in the build-up. So, signal for a goal, then blow for full time again and explain what happened to both captains. This messy end to the game could have been avoided had you given yourself another moment or two before calling time.

Page 84

201 You have to intervene here; you can't allow this to happen. The guidance is clear on this: equipment of this type (cameras, TV monitors, etc.) cannot be used in the technical area. Authorities can now impose retrospective punishments based on video evidence, but that does not mean teams can start filming each other from the dugout just in case. After the match, report what happened to the authorities.

202 In this scenario, the goal stands. Thank your assistant for taking responsibility and not immediately stopping the game, and confirm with him that the goal was valid. However, after this type of injury, you should relinquish your duties. It's not safe to continue after being knocked out – you should seek medical attention. Arrange for a colleague to step in.

203 You have no idea what substance is being injected, and you have no way of finding out. This player may be diabetic, so the injection may be perfectly legitimate. Have a word with the player, make sure the syringe is safely disposed of, and then allow him to enter the game as normal. Mention the incident in your post-match report.

Page 85

204 An embarrassing situation. Your red card is now valid only if the defender's challenge involved excessive force. Otherwise, call the defender back, explain the miscommunication to both captains, and restart with an indirect free kick for the offside offence You should show the defender a yellow card if his challenge was reckless.

205 The keeper must know he has committed an offence. He cannot handle a deliberate back pass. You must stop the game and award an indirect free kick to the attacking team. However, there is no case for a red card. A keeper is allowed to handle the ball, but not from a back pass. Don't forget to show the complaining captain a yellow card for his unsporting behaviour.

206 You're a referee not a doctor. Allow the injured player to stay on the pitch, in line with his team's wishes. But there are times when common sense means you have to intervene for player safety.

Page 86

207 Award a penalty kick and show the keeper a red card for denial of a goal-scoring opportunity. You should also show the defender a yellow card for unsporting behaviour. The game cannot restart without a goalkeeper, so a replacement must take his place.

208 There is no reason to stop him changing shirt so long as he's wearing a distinguishing colour. You should also check that the shirt has the same sponsor as his team.

209 Play on. It's unfortunate, but the ball striking the additional assistant referee is treated the same way as if the ball had struck you or any other 'fixture' on the field of play, such as a goalpost or corner flag.

Page 87

210 The stadium manager's idea might sound sensible – call for an early break and add an extra three minutes to the second half – but you cannot make up policy on the hoof. There are clear competition guidelines to make sure the right amount of time is played in the right format. So take the teams off, wait for the backup generators to kick in, then play the remaining three minutes before blowing for a normal half-time break. Report what happened to the authorities.

211 This is a clever trick, but you can't award the goal. Caution the player for unsporting behaviour. There is no way an opponent could have legally challenged for the ball. Restart with an indirect free kick at the point where he first managed to balance the ball.

212 You must base your decision on the expert medical advice, so you cannot award the goal. Play effectively stopped the moment the keeper had the seizure. Make sure the keeper is replaced (the game cannot resume without a player in goal) and restart with a dropped ball – on the six-yard line if he was inside the six-yard box when he collapsed.

Page 88

213 The attacking side may protest about this, but you should not take any action against the defender. This does not count as unsporting behaviour because, quite simply, the ball is not live until it leaves the area. So, while the defender may have used that law to avoid being in a difficult situation, he has not committed an offence. Have the keeper retake the goal kick.

214 Show two red cards. Clearly the striker is going to feel hard done by here, but his attempt to defend himself involved aggression and excessive force. Both players have committed red card offences, because attempting to strike an opponent warrants a dismissal whether or not contact is made.

215 The goal is valid. The referee is considered part of the field of play, so award the goal and restart the game in the usual way.

Page 89 Adam Lallana

216 There's no offence here. Players can eat anything they like during the game as long as it's a legal substance and they don't leave the pitch to do it. But if the wrappers are distracting your assistant, ask the stadium manager to have them cleared them away.

217 One quality a good official needs is humility when a mistake has been made. Apologise for this serious error, which has denied an innocent player a chance of an attempt on goal. Restart with a dropped ball from where it was when you stopped play, and have a word with your colleague.

218 An awful situation. The home side's anger and frustration is understandable, and you need to handle this carefully. Once security and medical staff have dealt with the incident, remind the home manager and captain that, however unfair it seems, the game cannot be completed without a nominated goalkeeper in place. Remind them that, if they refuse to put a player in goal, you will have no option but to abandon the game and report them, leaving the result, and their fate, entirely in the hands of the authorities.

Page 90

219 The player grabbed the post to avoid a potentially serious injury, and the ball hit him accidentally. Taking those factors into account, you cannot therfore view him as being guilty of unsporting behaviour. There has been no offence, the ball has deflected in off him in live play – so it's a goal.

220 Leaving the field without permission is an offence, but he may have had a legitimate, medical reason for doing so in a hurry. If this were the case, it would not be an automatic yellow card without further investigation. However, returning to the game without permission is definitely a bookable offence. In this case award a second yellow and send off the player.

221 This is clearly not acceptable: it's an offence to use a shirt like this, as it effectively becomes an extension of his hands. So the youngster has committed what counts as a deliberate handball on the line. However, his action has not prevented a certain goal, as the ball would have hit his body anyway. So it's a yellow card, a penalty, and a hard lesson learned.

Page 91

222 This is a simple call – no retake. The goalkeeper has failed to save a ball, which has hit the post and gone in. The flight of the ball was not altered by the puncture it sustained on hitting the frame of the goal, so the goal counts, and the result stands. The laws are explicit on this sort of scenario: only if the ball had clearly burst after being kicked, but before it hit the post, would you award a retake.

223 You can't agree to this. It's a competitive tournament and the rules have to be adhered to. This may not be the World Cup, but it's still important in any competition to make sure everything is fair. If the rules state extra time must be played, then it must be played, but you can, of course, allow water breaks.

224 Play on. You would stop the game only if the defender had been guilty of deliberate violent conduct. Fouls are penalised only if committed on opponents.

Page 92

225 What a mess. You have no option but to stop the shoot-out, apologise, and explain the situation to both teams, and blow for full time. Report your error to the authorities, and expect plenty of repercussions.

226 Safety is paramount, and shin guards are compulsory. That said, you should not disallow a goal because of your failure to enforce the laws. The player should not have been allowed to return without you checking his pads properly. This is a problem you have created, so allow the goal to stand, and ask the player to leave the field once again. This time, have a proper look before you allow him back on.

227 This is not only unsporting but also unsafe. There's a clear risk of injury here. At the next stoppage, caution the keeper for unsporting behaviour and restart in the normal way. He needs to show some respect.

Page 93

228 Mascots aren't above the laws of the game. Ask him or her politely to stay away from the pitch, explaining the problem. If the mascot won't budge, ask the stadium manager to intervene, and include it in your post-match report.

229 Yes, the goal stands. While this would be very unlikely to happen on a full-size pitch, it's not completely impossible on a smaller one. A goal can legitimately be scored with a keeper's punch from inside his own area.

230 First, make sure both players receive treatment. Then consult with your assistants and with the fourth official. If none of you saw the incident, you cannot act on it. You don't know why both players collapsed, you don't know when it happened – was it before the ball went in or after? You cannot make a guess. All you can do is act on the information you have, so award the goal, restart in the normal way and report what happened to the authorities. It's a clear case for video evidence to be used after the event.

Page 94

231 The defenders are right that stopping the ball leaving the area from a goal kick means that the kick has to be retaken, but this is clearly an unacceptable abuse of that law in an attempt to waste time. So have a word with the captain. Make it very clear to him that you will caution the next player who does this, and tell him you'll be adding time on to take account of the delays. That should sort it out.

232 First, you must restore order and deal with any injuries. Then show each of the twins a yellow card for removing their shirts. Next show one of them a red card for violent conduct. If you've got the right one, that's great. If not, and you've sent off the innocent twin, the authorities can deal with it after the match on appeal.

233 This is a foul. You cannot decide the outcome of a penalty kick until the ball has finished its natural course. In this case, the ball was clearly still spinning, and the keeper could have stopped it had he not been restrained. So, whatever the striker's motives, show him a yellow card for unsporting behaviour, disallow the goal, and allow the keeper's team to take the next kick.

Page 95

234 You should have been aware of who was, and was not, on the pitch before the kick was taken. As it is, you must disallow the goal, caution the scorer for re-entering the field of play without your permission, and allow one of his teammates to retake the penalty. The player must await to return to the pitch until you signal.

235 The rules governing a penalty shoot-out have changed to include this proviso: 'The referee must not abandon the match if a team is reduced to fewer than seven players during the taking of kicks from the penalty mark.' So no abandonment is possible – the shoot-out continues.

236 This is a mess. Try to calm everyone down, then take it step by step. Check that the boy is unhurt and make sure he is escorted away. Then show the striker a red card for committing a violent act, and the home captain a yellow card for unsporting behaviour. If you are satisfied that a goal would have been scored if the teenager had not intervened then award a goal. Include it all in your report.

Page 96

237 No goal. Once a kick is taken in a penalty shoot-out the taker has no further part to play – the outcome is determined when the ball has completed its path, with the keeper allowed to attempt a save. Had this been a penalty in open play, however, the taker would have been allowed to shield the ball like this – just as a defender might shepherd the ball out for a goal kick. Players are allowed to shield the ball so long as it is within playing distance of them.

238 If you allowed the player to start the match with this hairstyle – and there's no reason to bar a hairstyle unless it represents a potential danger – then there's nothing to stop him using it to his advantage. It's no more an offence than a clever ball juggler briefly balancing the ball on his head. Award the goal.

239 There's no need to disallow the goal – players are allowed to go off and on the field of play without permission if it's part of the same move to beat the opposition. So not only has the winger's pace spared his blushes with the awful first cross, he's managed to set up a perfectly valid goal, too.

Page 97

240 This is not a penalty as the ball is not in play. If you have not seen the incident and think he might be play-acting, take the injured player to one side with his captain. Remind them that you expect them to participate in the game in a fair manner. Ignore the appeals. If you have seen the incident, send off the defender for violent conduct. Either way, restart with the corner kick.

241 You cannot act on such comments at half time. However, as the referee, you are at fault here. You should have ensured before kick off that the goalkeeper is easily distinguished from his teammates and the opposition, and is wearing a jersey or shirt with long sleeves, which is now a requirement for all keepers.

242 The offence has occurred off the field, so stop play and caution the defender for unsporting behaviour, and restart play with a dropped ball. If you deem that the forward would have gained possession of the ball and being well ahead of the chasing pack, has been denied an obvious goal-scoring opportunity, send off the defender.

Page 98

243 You have to be aware of gamesmanship on both sides. Having rightly cautioned the striker for showing the imaginary card, you should then make sure you give him the appropriate protection to avoid this sort of escalation. Tell him that you're aware the opposition players are targeting him to try and force a second yellow. At the next opportunity take the opposition captain to one side and tell him to issue his team with a general warning that their tactic must stop. With that warning in place, you should then show a yellow card to the next player who fouls this individual.

244 The laws no longer recognise 'intent' as relevant when assessing a foul. In this case, the defender has committed a foul as a result of carelessness, however unintentional it may have been. Restart with a direct free kick, and show the defender a red card for the denial of an obvious goal-scoring opportunity.

245 Under no circumstances accept the shirt on the pitch – whatever the motivation. You could thank the captain for his wonderful gesture and suggest that, because you want to photograph the moment, he should keep his shirt on until you can do a formal presentation in your dressing room.

Page 99

246 Stay calm and think clearly. First disallow the goal, because a team cannot change a penalty taker once he has been identified. Second, show a yellow card to the player who took the kick. Restart the game with an indirect free kick to the opposition.

247 You can only award a penalty if you or your assistants saw a holding offence. But in any case, you should stop play. Once you have inspected the shirts, order the whole team – not just the three shirtless attackers – to replace their shirts and check them carefully. There might be sponsorship implications, but that's not your problem. Restart with a penalty if you saw any holding, or if not, with a dropped ball. After the game report what happened to the authorities.

248 Yes, you certainly should intervene. You had signalled for the corner to be taken, so the player has effectively kicked the replacement ball out for a goal kick. Speak to the player about his angry reaction and, if necessary, also ask his captain to tell him to calm down.

Page 100 Marta & Casey Stoney

249 You can only take action based on what you have seen. To punish a handball offence, you have to be sure it was deliberate, and you have to be able to identify the offender. Given that you were partly unsighted here, you can't make a sound judgement on either point. So, you have to award the goal.

250 The law allows a player to step off the pitch to avoid being involved in active play. But another view would be that at the time the free kick was taken, she was involved and trying to circumvent the law. The text quoted below from the rules seems to indicate that the situation described here cannot be considered legal. 'An attacking player may step or stay off the field of play not to be involved in active play. If the player re-enters from the goal line and becomes involved in play before the next stoppage in play, or the defending team has played the ball

towards the halfway line and it is outside their penalty area, the player shall be considered to be positioned on the goal line for the purposes of offside. A player who deliberately leaves the field of play and re-enters without the referee's permission and is not penalised for offside and gains an advantage, must be cautioned.
If an attacking player remains stationary between the goalposts and inside the goal as the ball enters the goal, a goal must be awarded unless the player commits an offside offence or Law 12 offence in which case play is restarted with an indirect or direct free kick.'

251 It's a clear case of denial of an obvious goal-scoring opportunity. But who to punish is less clear. Whenever offences are committed simultaneously, the advice to referees is to choose one of the offenders and show the individual a red card. So make your choice – ideally based on the severity of the challenges rather than who you like least – then award a penalty kick.

Page 101

252 Technically, yes, the player can stand where he likes during play – unless, of course, you award a restart, such as a free kick or corner where other players must be a certain distance from the ball, or at a kick-off after a goal, in which case every player must be inside his own half. But you also need to consider safety. Having an immobile player in the opposition area is a risk. So, call for medical attention, and make sure the injured player is removed from the field of play.

253 Deliberate handball covers a player's hand, forearm and the whole of his upper arm. However, although the ball was in contact with his upper arm, there is no offence committed here because the action by the defender was not deliberate. He may have jumped but he did not do so with his arms outstretched. Award a corner kick.

254 Award a corner. A goal cannot be scored from any free kick that is kicked directly into a team's own goal. The laws make clear that a corner should be awarded to the opposing team if this situation occurs.

Page 102 Sergio Aguero

255 The opponents are right. As things stand, the striker has to leave the field following treatment and await your signal to return after play resumes. He therefore cannot take the kick and another player must be nominated to take it. This rule unfairly punishes both him and his team, when they have done nothing wrong.

256 You cannot order substitutions, but you can encourage them. Explain to the manager and the player that vomit on the pitch represents a health risk to all players, and if it keeps happening, or it cannot be fully cleaned up and disinfected, you will have to abandon the game.

257 Both players are guilty of unsporting behaviour here, so show both a second yellow card, followed by reds. The striker's offence is obvious and the keeper should not be asking you to caution others – you are in charge, not him. Before restarting with a direct free kick to the defence – make sure another player goes in goal.

Page 103

258 What a nightmare. You and your colleagues count as part of the field of play, and normally if the ball makes contact with any of you, play continues. But in this case your assistant made a deliberate decision to pick up the ball and therefore directly interfered with play, so that rule does not apply. Stop the game, disallow the goal, and restart with a dropped ball from where he picked it up. When you do blow the final whistle, protect your colleague as you leave the field of play, and include the details in your report.

259 Childish, but then the manager should really have taken better care of his notes. Have a word with the player, advise him that he's neither big nor clever, and warn him about his future conduct. When you blow for half time, keep an eye on him and the manager to ensure the pair do not clash.

260 Assuming the eventual scorer also ran onto the ball from outside the area, award the goal. This hugely risky penalty routine is legal. But if the defender's challenge was reckless or used excessive force, issue a caution or send him off.

Page 104 Harry Kane

261 Take firm action. You have witnessed an aggressive, two-way confrontation, and you have evidence, based on the use of the word 'too', that the pair have traded racial insults. So show a red card to both and later file a detailed report. Quote what you heard, then leave it to the authorities to investigate the situation further.

262 Play on. Football is a contact sport and you should not be too quick to intervene and sanitise it, provided the keepers challenge was fair and not careless, reckless or involved excessive force. Players have a duty of care towards their opponents.

263 It can never be said too often – players have to play to the whistle. Whatever his reasoning, maybe that he didn't see or hear your signal, or that he just wanted a free kick instead, it's irrelevant. The player has committed an obvious offence. However, it's also the case that not every handball is an automatic yellow card – and this is probably an instance where a free kick is sufficient.

Page 105 Eric Dier

264 The attackers may see a corner as the best advantage you can give them in this situation, but its just not an option. The defender has committed two bookable offences in separate incidents, so the game stops there. Show him two yellow cards then a red, and restart with a direct free kick where the second offence was committed.

265 It is clear disrespect – an arrogant attempt to undermine your authority. Give him a final warning and remind him that officials are instructed to confirm all names to avoid the sort of errors that can arise when only numbers are recorded. If he continues to act up, show him a second yellow.

266 Yes, you can allow this. The substitution hasn't been completed until the departing player has stepped off the field of play and the replacement has stepped on. So the manager can reverse the change if he thinks that's the best way of handling the situation. Include what happened in your report.

Page 106

267 If the ball had hit an outside agent and deflected into the net, then that would mean a simple dropped-ball restart. But in this case, a clear offence has been committed – a deliberate attempt to influence play. So disallow the goal, show the player a yellow card for unsporting behaviour, and restart with an indirect free kick from the point on the goal area line, parallel to the goal line, nearest to where the snow made contact with the ball.

268 Play was still live, so award a penalty. If he has denied an obvious goal-scoring opportunity, send him off. And if the defender's original trip was reckless, show him a yellow card.

269 This issue is not covered in the laws, but it will be in the rules of the competition. If the name was offensive in some way, you should have him change the shirt; clubs are required to have spare, numberless shirts available in case a player has a blood injury and needs a replacement top. But in this case, let him continue and leave it to the authorities to decide on any action after the game.

Page 107 Willian

270 This is a textbook example of dissent. You have to stop play and show the away captain a yellow card. Restart with an indirect free kick to the attacking team on the goal area line parallel to the goal line, nearest to the position of the ball when play was stopped. This is all assuming, of course, that the ball was played forward from the kick off before the player embarked on this backwards dribble. If not, you will need to retake the kick off.

271 Nets are not compulsory according to the laws of the game, but most competitions require them in their rules. So ask a member of the ground staff to try to repair the net with tape. If this is impossible, play out the rest of the game, staying alert to the extra hole in the net. Ask the stadium manager to issue a stadium announcement to warn fans not to enter the field of play. Report what happened after the game.

272 The laws state: 'A player is not allowed to receive treatment on the field of play.' So it makes no difference whether the physio sprayed him or the player sprayed himself: he has to leave the pitch before play resumes. If he refuses, show him a yellow card for unsporting behaviour.

Page 108

273 Tempting as it may be, you can't show yourself a red card! You are considered part of the field of play and if the ball strikes you, it has to be accepted, just as if it had hit the corner flag. But of course, you should never deliberately play the ball. In this case, you must penalise the keeper – he has effectively played the ball twice, with no other player having touched it. Restart with an indirect free kick from where the keeper picked it up.

274 This is an obvious danger to himself and other players. Have him replace the boot and, if you know this is not the same boot he was wearing in the pre-match inspection, show him a yellow card for unsporting behaviour.

275 Stop the game and request a stadium announcement warning against this kind of chanting. If the chants continue, take the players off the field while the ground is cleared, then resume. Had the home side been winning 3–0, abandoning would have been a definite option. Report the matter to the authorities.

Page 109

276 Your response must be guided by what your assistant tells you, not what the players say, but use common sense here to calm the situation. Advise the player to keep his distance from your colleague for the rest of the game, and tell your assistant that you will be reporting what has happened to the authorities. Tell both that further incidents could lead to their removal.

277 You have to check these boots because any new equipment has to be approved by you. However, there is nothing in the laws prohibiting extra long boots or using padding. You can only check that the boots do not represent a danger. If you judge that they do, ask the player to replace them. These bizarre shoes may have given him an inch or two, but he must not move forward before the kick is taken.

278 Advise the player that your assistant has your full support. But discreetly, you can make sure that your colleague is patrolling the player's opposition attack to minimise potential flashpoints. Monitor the situation during the game and include the details in your post-match report.

Page 110

279 Play on, there's no reason to order a retake. No one is at fault here other than the penalty taker. He slipped and scuffed his shot. The fact that he did not directly make contact with the ball is irrelevant. It is enough that his kick caused the ball to move forward.

280 The managers are right to suspect that the authorities would order a replay in these circumstances, and their reluctance to go through it all again in a busy season is understandable. But it's your decision, not theirs. You need to judge it on the following grounds: whether there is enough visibility to avoid the shoot-out being a farce; whether there is any risk to player safety; whether it is reasonable to have the second half of the shoot-out played in very different conditions from the first; whether the paying public can see it properly. In most cases, it would be best to complete the shoot-out if at all possible, then leave it to the authorities to decide whether the result can stand.

281 You cannot go ahead. A size 5 ball is mandatory in senior football. Delay the restart in the hope that staff can recover one of the balls from outside the stadium, if this is not possible, you have to abandon the game.

Page 111

282 If you decide the noise was a deliberate attempt to distract the keeper, treat it as unsporting behaviour. Show the taker a yellow card and restart with an indirect free kick from the penalty mark. If not, award the goal. Professional keepers should be used to normal levels of noise during penalties.

283 It is not up to the teams, it is up to you – and your decision must be based on safety. Allow the game to go ahead only if you are happy that the artificial strip does not represent a danger to the players.

284 You have two options. Going by the letter of the law you should play on. You and your assistants are considered part of the field of play, like a goalpost or corner flag post, so if a player collides with you or an assistant, you play on. But to spare your assistant's blushes here, it may be advisable to stop play to check both are unhurt, then restart with a dropped ball.

Page 112 David de Gea

285 Your colleague has put you in an impossible position. However high-pressure a situation is, you and your officials have to stay calm and professional. As it is, you now have no choice but to dispense with your assistant's services and ask him to leave the field of play. Arrange for the fourth official to take over the line and organise a fourth official replacement. After the game, report the incident to the authorities.

286 It's a tough one, but you need to apply the law consistently. The striker has been denied an obvious goal-scoring opportunity, and while the defender's challenge was not deliberate, it was careless. Award a penalty and show the defender a red card.

287 Show him a second yellow card – followed by a red – for removing his shirt to celebrate a goal. It is irrelevant that this is a match behind closed doors, you need to apply the laws of the game consistently. In any case, if the stadium has a history of crowd trouble, the player's instinct to celebrate goals in a crowd-inciting way really needs to be stamped out.

Page 113 Martin O'Neill

288 Show the keeper a yellow card for delaying the restart. You are not there to help him defend his goal. If he comes out of his area to clear the ball, there is no reason for you to hold up play – or allow him to – while he gets back into position.

289 The law says that the goalposts and crossbar must be white, but in practice, you are advised to let the game go ahead anyway, even if replacement goalposts are not available. Playing with red and white posts will not affect the result, but postponing on a technicality would impact on fans, on fixture congestion, and on broadcasters. It is one of those situations where it's best left to the competition authorities to resolve.

290 You're in trouble. Had the ball been a regulation size 5 you could have ridden this situation out, awarded a penalty, sent the defender off and resumed with an official match ball. But in adult football, using a size 4 ball – which is at least five centimetres smaller in circumference – is not acceptable. Explain the situation to both teams, restart with a dropped ball on the six-yard line, and report what happened to the authorities. You can look forward to a break.

Page 114 Yaya Toure

291 Stop play. The midfielder needs to update his knowledge of the laws. He clearly thinks his teammate would be 'played on', but that's no longer the case. This is now considered a deflection, meaning that the player who has received the ball has gained it from an offside position. Restart with an indirect free kick for offside.

292 This may seem surprising, but the offence of 'back pass' is not mentioned in the laws – its just shorthand used by the media and fans. The laws provide more clarity, stating that a keeper cannot touch the ball with his hands after it has been kicked to him by a teammate. So, in this case the ball has been intercepted by the defender's foot, and deliberately left for the keeper to pick up. So stop the game and restart with an indirect free kick from where the keeper picked up the ball.

293 Put the wall back in its original position, respraying the foam line, if necessary, and do the same with the ball. Have a word with the kick-taker, too. It's not up to him where the kick is taken from – it's up to you. It's a good idea, when you position the ball for a free kick, to tell the taker that if he subsequently picks it up and moves it, he will be shown a yellow card for unsporting behaviour.

Page 115 Mick McCarthy

294 The guidance on this is clear – you can caution a player for taking off his shirt or lifting it over his face, only if he is celebrating, or deliberately inciting the crowd. So, in this case, just have a quiet word with the player. You'd only show him a yellow card if his behaviour delayed the restart.

295 The law defines how actions such as throw-ins should be carried out, but clearly you can make concessions for players with disabilities. Your ruling in this type of case must be based on fairness to all concerned.

296 The original keeper can take no further part and must leave the field of play. Allow the substitute keeper to return and replace him, and caution both for failing to inform you of the change. As for the restart, if the offending team have not had a goal scored against them since half time, restart the second half. If they have conceded, restart with an indirect free kick taken from where the ball was when you stopped play.

Page 116

297 You have to send the player off. However grateful you may feel, you have no alternative. In his intervention against the invading fan, the player has clearly committed an act of violent conduct and you have to stick to the laws. Obviously, you should clearly explain to him the reasoning behind your decision.

298 The actions of the goalkeeper need to be punished – he should have adjusted his tactics to the conditions. Award a direct free kick for his careless action. As for the condition of the pitch, you will need to keep monitoring it to ensure the safety of the players and to prevent the game from becoming a farce.

Page 117

299 It can go against every instinct, but players have to play to the whistle. This incident has happened at high speed and, while the keeper's reaction is understandable, players cannot decide when the game stops and starts – a power which could easily be misused for tactical gain. If you had spotted the injury instantly and whistled before the shot was taken it would be different. As it is, call for medical help, then award the goal.

300 This is a nightmare scenario and you need to act decisively. If you can pinpoint exactly when the extra player was brought on, speak to both captains and let them know you are restarting the game from that point, before this latest goal – and request a stadium announcement to relay the decision to the crowd. If you can't be sure when the extra player came on, or if one of the captains disagrees, allow the game to continue until full time. Either way, report everything that happened to the authorities.

Index of offences and issues

Acknowledgements

First I would like to thank my valued friend and the other half of the *You Are The Ref* conundrums for his unchallengeable knowledge of the laws of our beautiful game. Keith Hackett's concise explanation of every refereeing decision in this book has inspired the artist's brush. To Trevor Davies, for his wisdom and foresight in stressing the need for the VAR system to be illustrated and explained in the book. This will enable the football world to understand VAR more fully, and will provide the insight for the technology to be embraced. Special thanks also to my computer literate wife, Lorraine Trevillion, whose digital knowhow ensured all the content in this book arrived safely with the expert creatives at Octopus and last but not least, my Literary Agent Rick 'The Colonel' Mayston of Agent Fox Media – the man who made the *You Are The Ref* book a reality.

Paul Trevillion

I would like to thank Rod Pelosi, Joe Guest, Ted Kearney and James Finnegan for their continued friendship and dialogue on refereeing matters over many years.

Keith Hackett